Isabel Allende

Award-Winning Latin American Author

MARY MAIN

Enslow Publishers, Inc.

40 Industrial Road   PO Box 38
Box 398   Aldershot
Berkeley Heights, NJ 07922   Hants GU12 6BP
USA   UK

http://www.enslow.com

Dedication
For Jenna and Megan Disney,
follow your dreams

Acknowledgment
Heartfelt thanks to Donna Brown Agins, fellow author,
for her patience, support, and friendship.

Library of Congress Cataloging-in-Publication Data

Main, Mary.
 Isabel Allende : award-winning Latin American author / Mary Main.
  p. cm. — (Latino biography library)
 Includes bibliographical references and index.
 ISBN-10: 0-7660-2488-1 (hardcover)
  1. Allende, Isabel. 2. Authors, Chilean—20th century—Biography. I. Title. II. Series.
PQ8098.1.L54Z76   2005
863'.64—dc22

2004027541

ISBN-13: 978-0-7660-2488-5

Printed in the United States of America

10 9 8 7 6 5 4 3 2

To Our Readers:
We have done our best to make sure all Internet Addresses in this book were active and
appropriate when we went to press. However, the author and the publisher have no control over
and assume no liability for the material available on those Internet sites or on other Web sites they
may link to. Any comments or suggestions can be sent by e-mail to comments@enslow.com or to
the address on the back cover.

Every effort has been made to locate all copyright holders of material used in this book. If any
errors or omissions have occurred, corrections will be made in future editions of this book.

Illustration Credits: © Isabel Allende Archives, pp. 6, 12, 16, 18, 25, 40, 43, 45, 51, 53, 82, 91;
© Lori Barra, p. 4; © William Gordon, pp. 27, 76, 81, 85, 86, 90; AP/Wide World, pp. 1, 3, 32, 52,
58, 65, 67, 70, 72, 88, 97, 103; Artville LLC, pp. 14, 29, 42; Enslow Publishers, Inc., p. 101.

Cover Illustration: © William Gordon.

Contents

Isabel Allende

Help From
the Spirits

Far from her home in Santiago, Chile, Isabel Allende received the news that her grandfather was gravely ill. It was January 1981, and her beloved Tata (Grandpa) was nearly one hundred years old. Allende worried that he would die soon. Yet she would not go back to Chile as long as the military dictatorship ruled the country. If she returned, she feared she would be imprisoned, tortured, or even killed. Then Allende remembered something her grandfather had told her. He said that people only truly die when they are forgotten.[1] Allende decided to write her grandfather a letter filled with family stories.

At that time, Allende was living with her husband and two children in an apartment in Caracas, Venezuela. Her mother and stepfather lived upstairs on the third floor. An uproar of traffic and street violence poured in through the windows. The apartment felt like a prison. Allende said she longed for "the peace of a forest, the silence of a mountain, the whisper of the sea" in her native Chile.[2]

The days were long. Allende worked a double shift at her job as a school administrator, arriving at seven in the morning and working until seven at night. Then she ate dinner with her family. On the evening of January 8, 1981, Allende set up her portable typewriter to begin her letter to Tata. She wrote late into the night. As words flowed through her fingers, her homesickness was transformed into energy and enthusiasm.

When Allende started writing a letter to her beloved grandfather, she had no idea it would become her first novel.

Allende began her letter with the story of her grandfather's first love, a beautiful and mysterious great-aunt who had died from poisoning. Then Allende added even more intrigue to the family history. She created a woman with white skin, green hair, and gold eyes who looked like a mermaid. She named her Rosa. In Rosa the Beautiful's character, family truths mingled with traits from Allende's imagination.[3] The letter was turning

6

into something Allende had not expected. It was turning into a novel. Allende had spent twenty years as a journalist and playwright in Chile. She could not imagine herself as a novelist. In fact, the idea seemed a bit arrogant, although she was having too much fun to stop.

Every day, Allende tied a ribbon around her manuscript and took it to work in a canvas satchel, keeping it close to her. At night, she sat at her typewriter and let the story pour out onto the paper. Even the news that Tata had died did not dampen her enthusiasm for writing. Allende felt the spirits of her grandparents in the room, guiding her words. She believed that Memé and Tata were helping her create the exciting saga of the del Valle and Trueba families.

The Novel

A novel is a book of fiction in which the author creates characters and events. The word *novel* comes from Renaissance Italy, where it was used to describe a realistic tale. Medieval romance stories were another form of the early novel and often included supernatural events. During the 1800s, the novel became the most popular form of literature, and many countries produced great novelists, such as Jane Austen from England, Victor Hugo from France, and Leo Tolstoy from Russia. There have been many famous American novelists, including Mark Twain and Ernest Hemingway.

> *As she wrote, Allende felt the spirits of her grandparents in the room, guiding her words.*

Allende spiced up her story with wacky events. In one scene, Uncle Marcos builds a giant bird and flies off over a mountain range. A week after the family mourns at his funeral, he comes walking out of the mountains, happy and healthy.

In another scene, the character Clara searches for her mother's head—severed from her body in a car crash. Clara finds the head by the side of the road, looking like a "lonely melon."[4] She hides it in a leather hatbox in the basement. Twenty years later, the family finds it and sets it next to Clara in her coffin.

Allende drew on actual events in her own life to create many of her scenes. Two events inspired the severed head incident. The first is that Allende had a friend whose parents were killed in a car crash, and the mother was decapitated in the accident. The sons had to retrieve the head from under some bushes. The other incident was from Allende's childhood. After she found a skull in the basement of her grandfather's house, she started using it in some of her games.

Because Allende combines real events with imaginative ways of looking at the world, her writing is known as "magical realism."[5] Strange and supernatural events are incorporated into her books as though they actually happened.[6] To Allende, magic realism is "something mysterious or difficult to explain that happens in real life—ESP, premonitions, prophetic dreams, incredible coincidences."[7]

One day, Allende realized that she had written five hundred pages. It was time to end her novel, but how? She was stumped for ideas until Tata came to her in a dream to give her the answer. In the dream, Allende approached the bed where her grandfather slept. When she picked up the sheet, she saw that he was dead. This dream gave her the idea of having the granddaughter in the book sit beside the body of her grandfather as she tells the story. Allende woke from the dream at three o'clock in the morning. She hurried to the kitchen and typed a ten-page epilogue without stopping.

Allende's mother helped choose the title *The House of the Spirits* and persuaded Allende to try to publish the book. They sent letters to publishers, but no one wrote back. Finally, Allende heard about a literary agent in Barcelona, Spain. A literary agent advises authors and helps sell their books to publishing houses. Allende mailed the manuscript to Carmen Balcells. Within weeks she received a telephone call: Balcells wanted to be her agent. Six months later, *The House of the Spirits* was published in Spain, with an image of green-haired Rosa the Beautiful on the cover.

In Madrid, Spain, Balcells threw a lavish party for Allende. All the celebrities in Spanish literary circles were there. Allende could not believe she deserved such recognition. How would she talk to all these brilliant people? "I was so frightened I spent a good part of the evening hiding in the bathroom," she said later.[8]

Allende finally gained confidence and enjoyed the fame her novel brought her. In 1985, *The House of the Spirits* was translated into English and published in the United States by the respected publishing house Alfred A. Knopf. The novel became an international best-seller. Isabel Allende had taken the literary world by storm. She said writing *The House of the Spirits* was like opening a floodgate and letting out a torrent: "I never recovered from the tremendous impact of that torrent. It changed my life."[9]

In the midst of sadness and separation from her grandfather and her beloved homeland of Chile, Isabel Allende penned one of the most popular family sagas of the twentieth century and was propelled to international success.[10] Isabel Allende the journalist could now think of herself as a novelist.

2

House of Shadows

Isabel Allende was born on August 2, 1942, in Lima, Peru. Although her parents were from Chile, they were living in Peru. Her father, Tomás Allende, was Secretary of the Chilean Embassy. Her mother, Francisca Llona Barros Allende, was a homemaker. Isabel and her two younger brothers, Francisco (called Pancho) and Juan, were all born in Peru.

World War II was raging across Europe and the Pacific at the time of Isabel's birth. American soldiers were fighting with the Allied Forces of Great Britain and the Soviet Union against Japan and Germany. Although much of the world was unstable then, World War II did not reach Latin America, where Isabel's family lived.

In 1945, when Isabel was three years old, her parents separated. The Chilean consul in Peru, a man named Ramón Huidobro, helped Francisca book passage on a boat leaving Peru. Francisca gathered her three children,

Isabel, about a year old, with her mother and newborn brother Francisco in Lima, Peru.

their nanny Margara, and their dog Pelvina López-Pun, and sailed home to Chile. Isabel never spoke to her father, Tomás Allende, again. All photographs of him were burned, and his name was never mentioned.[1] When Isabel asked questions about him, she was told only that he was a very intelligent gentleman.[2]

Chile is a Catholic country with strict religious beliefs, and at that time divorce was forbidden. Isabel's mother had her marriage annulled by the Catholic Church, which declared that a valid marriage never existed. Many people criticized Francisca for ending her unhappy marriage, but her family supported her decision. Her relatives had never approved of the marriage between Francisca and Tomás, because he was fifteen years older than she and did not embrace the family's religious beliefs.[3]

The change from protected wife to single mother was not easy for Isabel's mother. Francisca Allende, known as "Panchita," had been raised in an affluent home and admired as the most beautiful girl in her family. Growing up, she spent her time going to school, reading romantic novels, and doing charitable works. She had lived a privileged life. After the separation from her husband, Panchita had come home to her family in Chile.

Chile resembles a long, thin, winding ribbon along the southwest coast of South America. The country stretches 2,700 miles from top to bottom, equal to the distance from San Francisco to New York, and is no

Isabel's roots are in Chile, but she has lived in many different countries.

wider than 150 miles. It is a land of lush valleys, soaring mountains, and wild seas. Earthquakes, volcanic eruptions, and floods occur regularly. The climate is a study in contrasts, hot in the northern deserts and often cold and rainy in the south. There are also many mild days, much like the weather in California.

At home in Santiago, three-year-old Isabel, her mother, and her brothers moved into her grandparents' colonial-style home on Suecia Street. Heavy, dark furniture, considered the finest of its time, decorated the house. Dark red upholstery covered the sofas and chairs that filled the drafty rooms. A grand piano and a crystal chandelier dominated the living room. When the huge black grandfather clock struck the hour, it sounded like funeral bells to Isabel.[4] In spite of its gloomy furnishings, the house was lively, filled with exotic animals, visitors, and music.

Isabel's grandfather Agustín Llona Cuevas was a successful businessman. He provided everything his family needed. A staff of servants cared for Tata and the rest of the family, including Isabel's two uncles who lived with them. Isabel's grandfather was extremely religious and conservative. He believed that men were superior to women and children and must guide and protect them. This belief is known as patriarchy. As a self-made man and the patriarch of the family, Tata had many strong opinions. He taught Isabel that life is hard and that the highest goal is success.[5]

Isabel's grandmother Isabel Barros Moreira, who

Did Isabel's grandmother Memé really have special powers?

was known as Memé, was believed to possess extrasensory powers. She often met with her friends, the three Mora sisters, to hold spiritual séances. It was said that Memé could send the sugar bowl skittering across the table and predict future events.

A small silver bell, its handle shaped like a silver prince, sat at Memé's place at the dinner table. Once, after a dinner party, Isabel claimed that she and the guests had watched, awestruck, as the bell slid across the tablecloth, made a wide turn, and then returned to Memé's place at the foot of the table.[6]

The world with its meanness, violence, and vulgarity was often too much for Memé. At those times, Isabel's grandmother retreated from life to roam the halls, lost in her own dreamy silence.[7] Memé refused to dial a telephone and said she used mental telepathy to exchange recipes with the Mora sisters on the other side of the city. She spent the majority of her time visiting the slums to help people, sewing, and collecting money for the poor.

When Memé died from leukemia, the house sank

into mourning. Tata wore all black clothing and insisted that everyone else in the house do the same. He had the furniture painted black and gave the order that there would be no parties, music, flowers, or desserts. He eliminated anything that might bring cheer to the household and disturb his grief for his beloved wife. Silence spread through the house, and it became a dark, ugly, cold place for Isabel.[8] She imagined that spirits haunted the corridors and that Satan lived inside the mirrors.

At that time, there was no television in Chile, and Tata did not allow the radio turned on very often. To ease her unhappiness, Isabel escaped into stories. Books overflowed the shelves and desk of her uncle Pablo's room, providing an instant library for the curious young girl. Since her grandfather had a strict rule of lights out at nine o'clock, Uncle Pablo gave her a flashlight. She hid books under the covers to read at night. Adventure stories and detective novels were her favorites. She also devoured Spanish translations of sophisticated novels such as *Anna Karenina* and *Les Miserables*. Her uncle rewarded her with a doll when she completed *War and Peace*. As she read, she longed for romantic and violent things to happen in the stories.[9]

The cellar of the big house was a wonderful place to escape. There Isabel played make-believe games, reading by candlelight, dreaming of magic castles, and dressing up like a ghost. Her active imagination led her to use an entire series of discarded books to build forts. She would then fall asleep in her imaginary kingdom.

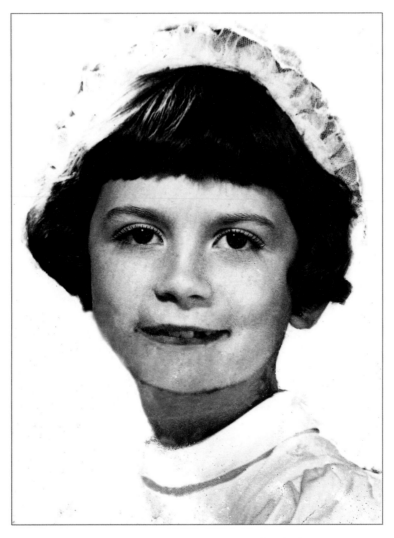

From an early age, Isabel, shown here in 1950, became an enthusiastic reader with a wild imagination.

In the cellar Isabel also found a trunk filled with books abandoned by her father. The trunk was the only proof Isabel had ever seen that her father existed. Novels written by Jules Verne, Emilio Salgari, Charles Dickens, and other authors filled the trunk. Captivated by the mystery surrounding her father, Isabel read the books voraciously. Yet her questions about her father remained unanswered.

To ease her unhappiness, Isabel escaped into stories.

Isabel's mother, Panchita, found a full time job at a local bank but did not earn enough money to support her children without help from Uncle Pablo and Tata. Panchita supplemented her income by making and selling beautiful hats. All the stress of trying to make ends meet gave her terrible headaches that sent her to bed for two or three days at a time. Isabel was terrified her mother would die and she would be sent to live with her father. Since it was forbidden to speak about her father, she could not tell anyone about her fears.[10]

Margara, the children's nanny, took control. If the children disobeyed her orders, she hit them with a leather strap. Isabel later described Margara as a tyrant who tried to separate the children from their mother. She would bathe, feed, and put the children to bed before Panchita came home from work. If Isabel and her brothers were still awake when their mother arrived, Magara ordered them not to disturb her.

Often, Isabel and her brothers ignored Magara and

tiptoed into their mother's room at night. There, the three children listened with rapt attention as Panchita told them stories about their ancestors. In Panchita's imaginary world, everyone was happy. These family times inspired a love of storytelling in Isabel.[11]

Isabel began making up her own stories. She loved to torture her brothers with horrifying tales that scared them so much they could not sleep. Making things up— lying—is part of storytelling, but Isabel did not think of her stories as lies. Stories are created to entertain; lies are meant to deceive. Just the same, she would often be punished for lying.

Life was not all sad and gloomy. Panchita recognized her daughter's gift for creativity and allowed Isabel to paint whatever she wanted on the walls of her room. Isabel painted friends, animals, and landscapes. On an occasional Sunday, the family would trek to the top of San Cristóbal, a hill in the center of the city. Salvador Allende Gossens, a cousin of Isabel's father, and his wife, Hortensia, sometimes joined them with their three daughters and their dogs. Salvador Allende was a doctor and a well-known socialist politician in Chile. Isabel called him "Uncle Salvador." On those Sunday afternoons, the family picnicked on chicken and hard-boiled eggs and played games. Still, even these pleasant times were tinged with the dark side. Roars of lions from the city zoo echoed through the hillside as the big cats were fed live animals. Isabel and her cousins imagined that dinner for the lions came from the animal shelter, and they cringed in horror at the roars.[12]

Isabel was still very young when Tata took her to visit Patagonia in the south to watch sheep being sheared of their wool. It was a rough trip, and Isabel was violently carsick. Once they arrived at their destination, mules carried them over mountain passes into the wilderness. Isabel was thrown to the ground twice. But she was enchanted by the huge ferns and tree trunks and snow-covered volcanoes in the high mountain passes. Her love for her homeland of Chile grew even stronger on this trip.

Isabel loved to torture her brothers with horrifying tales that scared them so much they could not sleep.

The sheep shearing shocked Isabel with its cruelty. The workers were paid by the animal. The faster they sliced the wool off the sheep, the more money they earned. Sometimes strips of the animal's skin came off along with the wool. The bleeding animal was then stitched up and returned to the herd in the hopes it would survive.

In the evenings, the herdsmen would kill a lamb and roast it on a spit. Isabel and Tata sat with the men. They ate the roasted meat and washed it down with *mate*, a green, bitter tea served in a gourd. The herdsmen passed the gourd around, and everyone sipped from the same metal straw. By the time the gourd came to Isabel,

Patagonia

Patagonia is a huge area at the southern end of South America. It is three times the size of California. Vast empty spaces, lush green forests, and snow-capped mountains make up this land at what has been called the end of the world. On the western border, between Chile and Argentina, the soaring Andes protect the land from Pacific storms.

Many Europeans immigrated to Patagonia in the 1800s, and English is still spoken in many towns. Sheep raising is a key industry. Many of the sheep stations are run by descendants of the original immigrants. Patagonia is a popular destination for hikers, bicyclists, mountain climbers, and others who love the outdoors.

the straw was slippery with spit and chewing tobacco. But she had to take her turn. To refuse would have been bad manners and an insult to the herders.

Isabel's family spent summers at the shore, where they owned a huge, damp house. At that time, the car trip took a whole day. The entire family, including the parrot and the dog, Pelvina López-Pun, made the trip in Tata's black English touring car. Isabel and the others suffered terrible carsickness on those rides. But once at the shore, Isabel forgot about her nausea. La Playa Grande was beautiful. Children played on the beach all morning with nannies and mothers. Margara tied the children to her with ropes so they could safely splash in the water while she knit sweaters and Isabel's mother sunbathed. At two o'clock, they all went home for lunch and a siesta.

At the end of the day, Panchita would take Isabel's hand and lead her to a place where they could watch the sunset. There, one day, she told Isabel that she was in love with a man named Ramón Huidobro. He was a diplomat who worked in the embassy in Peru—the man who had helped the family return to Chile after Panchita left Isabel's father. Isabel imagined Huidobro as an enchanted prince living in a far-off land in a fairy tale. She was glad he lived far, far away.[13]

Back in Santiago, Isabel was surprised one day when Ramón Huidobro came to visit. Convinced that he was imaginary, she could hardly believe he was a real person and was in love with her mother. Far from the handsome prince of her fantasies, Isabel thought the real Ramón was the ugliest man she had ever seen. Fear gripped Isabel. Would her mother marry Ramón and abandon Isabel and her brothers?[14]

Isabel's fears of abandonment did not come true. Still, the man she would come to call Tío Ramón (Uncle Ramón) would change her life in many ways.

3

Adíos to Suecia Street

In 1952, when Isabel was ten years old, her mother and Tío Ramón decided to marry. Tío Ramón was assigned as a diplomat to the country of Bolivia. Panchita and her three children would go with him to the city of La Paz.

A highly sensitive and creative child, Isabel often exaggerated events and allowed her imagination to liven things up. On her last night in her grandfather's house, she crept downstairs into the drawing room, where she believed Memé's spirit waited for her in the heavy drapes. According to Isabel, Memé told her to retrieve a silver mirror from the master bedroom and take it with her to Bolivia. Every time Isabel looked into the mirror, Memé would be there with her. Isabel crept upstairs into the big dark bedroom where her grandfather slept. Terrified that he would wake, she searched through bureau drawers until she found the mirror. Back in bed, she peered into the glass, halfway expecting

Isabel's mother told wonderful stories and encouraged her creativity.

to see a demon, for she had been told that evil creatures lived in mirrors. Instead, in her imagination, she saw Memé telling her good-night.[1]

Early the next morning, Isabel added the word *adíos* (good-bye) to the mural on her bedroom wall. The family spent the day packing suitcases and tying them on top of the cars they would drive to the port. They would take a ship, then a train high into the Andes Mountains. Isabel was leaving her home, her country, and her beloved grandfather to travel to an unknown place. Tata stood in the doorway, dressed all in black, waving good-bye. She felt as if her childhood ended at that moment.[2]

On the journey, Panchita gave Isabel a notebook and suggested she write about her travels. Isabel wrote about all the sights, sounds, and smells she experienced on the way to Bolivia. Writing in the notebook helped Isabel understand her feelings and gave her a sense of what was real. From that time on, Isabel has written in her notebook nearly every day. She says it helps her "sort out the confusion of life."[3]

> *Tata stood in the doorway, dressed all in black, waving good-bye. She felt as if her childhood ended at that moment.*

La Paz was a beautiful city high in the Andes Mountains. The family moved into a compound of three houses that shared a common garden. In the quiet of the garden, Isabel found hiding places for her notebook

Panchita and Tío Ramón, Isabel's mother and stepfather.

and some hideouts where she could read and write in solitude.

One day at Isabel's new school, the teacher said that soldiers from Chile had committed brutal acts against the people of other countries during wartime. Isabel had always believed that her country was the best in the world. She was sure that her country would never do bad things. When she spoke up, the teacher ordered her to stand in the hallway.[4] Isabel stood there, fighting back tears. After a few minutes, she noticed she was not the only one being punished. A dark-haired boy with very large ears stood in the opposite corner, his face to the wall.

Isabel developed a crush on the boy and began writing stories about him in her notebooks. He ignored Isabel, acting as if she did not exist. The other kids in school knew she liked the boy with the big ears and made fun of her. Isabel's first crush ended in unexpected chaos. One day she and the boy ended up in a big fight on the playground. Isabel bit the boy's ear. Far from being upset about it, Isabel enjoyed the tussle.[5]

Shortly after Isabel's fight with the boy, Tío Ramón was given another diplomatic position, this time in Beirut, Lebanon. Isabel and her family had to move once again.

Isabel had mixed feelings about Tío Ramón but would eventually come to think of him as her true father.[6] He believed in training children to be strong and independent. He taught Isabel and her brothers that they should have goals and move steadily toward those goals.[7] Tío Ramón gave Isabel the complete works of William Shakespeare as a gift. She read Shakespeare's plays over and over, just as other kids read comic books. The stories of murderous kings and passionate lovers fired up her imagination and prepared her for the writer she would one day become. "I would draw the characters on cardboard, cut them out, paste a stick behind them and act out the plays," she said later.[8]

In 1955, when Isabel was twelve years old, Tío Ramón flew to Paris en route to his new post in Beirut. Isabel and her brothers traveled back home to Chile with their mother, then to Genoa and Rome, Italy. From Rome, they went to Beirut to rejoin Tío Ramón. The journey took two months.

In Beirut, the family lived in a big apartment. Isabel would often sit at the window of the apartment, peering at the activities in the streets below. There she saw automobiles and camels and fancy Cadillacs driven by rich sheikhs. There were Muslim women dressed all in black, totally

When Isabel's stepfather became a diplomat in Lebanon, the family moved to the Middle East.

covered except for a peephole for their eyes. Enchanted by the music, sounds, and smells of the city, she felt as if she were locked away in a prison.[9]

Beirut was a busy and fascinating place. At that time, it was considered the Paris of the Middle East, the center of culture and business. Several times a day, Isabel heard the high, wailing sounds of the religious men calling the faithful to prayer along with bells chiming atop Christian churches. Isabel would often shop with her mother in the souks—narrow alleyways lined with shops selling everything from food to clothing to antiques. Every aroma imaginable wafted from the alleys. Delicious smells of exotic foods and perfumes mingled with the stink of garbage and sewage floating in open drains.

Isabel's mother had a difficult time adjusting to the culture and hot weather in Lebanon. She also wished her family were rich like the other diplomats' families. Still, Panchita made the best of her circumstances, sewing herself a beautiful dress to wear to diplomatic events. She decorated the apartment with paintings from the house in Chile and tapestries purchased on credit in Beirut. Silver trays from home were used to serve food to guests. But the beautiful surroundings were not always peaceful. Panchita and Tío Ramón argued a lot; their quarrels often lasted until both parents were exhausted.[10]

Isabel attended an English private school for girls. Her friends at school had never heard of Chile and thought she came from China.[11] The school was very strict. The teachers trained Isabel and her classmates to control their emotions. Slight surprise was the only emotion allowed. All the girls had to memorize the Bible. When Isabel's teacher, Miss St. John, called out a chapter and verse number, the girls were expected to recite the verse immediately. This exercise improved Isabel's English. She also learned to speak French.

The school uniforms had been designed for the cool foggy weather of England, not the heat and humidity of Beirut. The girls wore heavy, clunky-looking shoes and helmet-style hats that covered their foreheads. Their dresses were long tunics made out of coarse cloth. Buttons were considered a luxury, so the girls tied their uniforms closed with strings.

Every day the girls ate unsalted rice. Depending on the day of the week, vegetables, yogurt, or boiled liver accompanied the rice. Despite the strict discipline, ugly uniforms, and boring food, Isabel liked the school's structure. Like a port in a storm, it gave her a safe haven from her chaotic home life. The school's challenges trained her to never give up when faced with life's obstacles.

Isabel's classmates came from all over the world, and most of them lived at the school. Shirley, the prettiest girl in the school, was from India. She taught Isabel how to belly dance. When Shirley was fifteen years old, she was taken out of school and sent back to India, where her parents had arranged a marriage for her.

When fighting broke out in the streets of Beirut, Isabel's family hid inside their apartment.

In July 1958, the political unrest in the Middle East erupted in violence. Tío Ramón ordered Isabel and her brothers to place mattresses in front of the windows because stray bullets could shatter the glass. He forbade them to step outside their third-floor apartment. Still, the children would sneak onto the balcony to watch gun battles in the streets below. Isabel and her brothers observed many horrific acts. Once, the corpse of a man with a slit throat was left in the street for two days.[12] The battles often lasted most of the day. When night came, the fighting would stop.

The political crisis came to a head when the United States Marine Corps sent a fleet to Lebanon in July 1958 in an attempt to restore peace to the Middle East. Isabel was fifteen years old. At an indoor skating rink, she skated among young men dressed in the uniforms of United States Marines. Their slang was quite different

The 1958 Beirut Uprising

In 1958, Beirut was wracked by internal revolts. A brutal coup had taken place in nearby Iraq, and violence broke out on the border of Lebanon and Syria. Lebanon's president, Camille Chamoun, sent an urgent request to U.S. President Dwight D. Eisenhower asking for help in fighting the Lebanese rebels. In response, Eisenhower dispatched thousands of U.S. Marines to Lebanon to restore the peace and preserve the government.

from the formal English she had heard at school. One of the Marines skated up to Isabel, kissed her on the lips, and skated off. Isabel was not sure which man it was, because with their short hair and tattoos, they all looked alike to her. She decided she would like to try kissing again. It would not be soon, however. Tío Ramón ordered Isabel to stay in the house.

Despite the warring in the streets, Isabel's school stayed open. The other schools closed, and her brothers stayed home. Isabel was thankful she could go to school and escape the boredom of the house. Eventually, though, so many parents removed their children from the school that Miss St. John was forced to close its doors. The government told diplomats to send their families home because it could not protect them from the violence. Tío Ramón arranged for Isabel and her brothers to leave on one of the last commercial flights out of the city. Panchita stayed with him in Beirut. Isabel was on her way home to Chile without her mother.

On the plane, Isabel wrote a letter to her mother. From then on, no matter where she was in the world, she would write to her mother every day. The habit played a vital role in Isabel's growth as a writer.[13]

Isabel was beginning to feel the uncontrollable rebelliousness that would prompt so many of her choices later in life.[14]

4

Return to
Suecia Street

When they returned to Chile in 1958, Isabel and her brothers were reunited with their grandfather in the house on Suecia Street. Tata had put away his mourning clothes and married a tall, dignified lady who was an excellent cook and housekeeper. Isabel soon learned that her parents had been assigned as diplomats to Turkey and would not be coming home to Chile for some time.

Because of the family's travels, Isabel's education had been quite unstructured. Spanish was her primary language, and she spoke some English and French. Books had been her constant companions for her entire life, and she was well read in fine literature as well as popular fiction. At Miss St. John's school, she had memorized many Bible verses. Still, according to her grandfather, her education was far from complete.

Tata decided that Isabel could finish her schooling

in a year if she attended high school and was tutored by him in history and geography. She was enrolled in La Maisonette, another exclusive school for girls. When Tata found out that Isabel had never learned mathematics, he signed her up for private classes with a math tutor.

Tata had little patience in his teaching sessions. Mistakes made him angry, but if Isabel did well, he rewarded her with a wedge of Camembert cheese from his armoire.[1] Isabel and Tata enjoyed each other's company and could sit together for hours without talking. Sometimes they read. Other times they listened with glee to horror shows on the radio. During this time, Isabel devoured science fiction books. She and her grandfather grew very close.[2]

Tata's new wife entertained relatives—including Salvador Allende and his family—every Sunday evening. She was fond of the family, and she never intruded on Isabel's time with her grandfather.

In 1959, sixteen-year-old Isabel passed an exam to receive her high school diploma. Although her grades qualified her to study at the university, she decided not to go to college. At that time Chilean women did not pursue careers. Isabel expected to marry, have children, and become a housewife like most of the women she knew. Her plan seemed to be right on track when she fell in love with a handsome twenty-year-old engineering student named Miguel Frías.

Allende was confused about what to do while Frías

finished his university education. Tío Ramón advised her to work for a year. Isabel took his advice and got a job as a secretary at the Food and Agriculture Organization, a specialized agency of the United Nations. The FAO aimed to help agricultural workers and to improve nutrition worldwide. Allende's job involved copying forestry statistics, and she found the work boring.[3]

Allende also worked translating English romance novels into Spanish. In most of these novels, the heroes were superior to the heroines. Allende thought the

United Nations

The name United Nations was coined by President Franklin D. Roosevelt. On January 1, 1942, twenty-six countries joined in the Declaration by United Nations in fighting World War II. In 1945, immediately after the war, the United Nations Charter was established, setting out the organization's policy and structure. Keeping peace among the nations of the world was the major goal of the United Nations. The organization also aimed to solve international economic, social, cultural, and humanitarian problems. Although its peacekeeping efforts have not always been successful, the United Nations—which today has 191 member countries—remains a forum for debate among the nations of the world.

heroines in these stories seemed stupid. Sometimes she changed the heroine's dialogue to make the character sound more intelligent. She also added to the stories' endings so that the heroine became independent of the hero and did some good in the world. Allende was going beyond the role of a translator—and she was fired from the job.

When Allende's parents returned from Turkey, she moved into their Spanish-style colonial home on the outskirts of Santiago. Every day at dawn, Allende rose, dressed, and caught the bus to the city. In the evenings after work, the buses were full, so she began stopping off at her grandfather's house to wait for a later bus. Soon she was visiting her grandfather every day for tea and conversation.

Allende has called her relationship with her grandfather "enraged intimacy" because the two had so many arguments about politics and the roles of women.[4] Tata believed that men were superior to women in every way, and because women were helpless, men should take care of them. He believed that women should stay home and take care of the house while men pursue careers. His beliefs sprang from a world view known as *machismo* in Spanish.

Allende rebelled against Chile's system of patriarchy. She did not intend to live her life at the whims of men. She refused to become a dependent victim, as she believed her mother had been. She demanded her grandfather's respect. Both of them were stubborn in their opinions. Despite their many disagreements, Isabel and her grandfather loved each other deeply.

Tata told Isabel stories about his life, too, and Isabel loved listening to him talk.[5] She was fascinated by the way he had lived. His memories brought the past to life for her, and she later tried to recreate her grandfather's world in *The House of the Spirits*. Her grandfather was a constant source of inspiration. "My daily visits with Tata provided me with enough material for all the books I have written, possibly for all I will ever write," she said later.[6]

On September 8, 1962, at the age of twenty, Isabel Allende married Miguel Frías. Because her father was absent from her life, Uncle Salvador stood in for him at the wedding. In an unusual move for her culture, she did not add her husband's last name to her own. Using only her own name was a symbol of her anger at the idea that men held the power in society.[7]

> *"My daily visits with Tata provided me with enough material for all the books I have written."*

When Panchita and Tío Ramón were assigned to Switzerland, they left their beautiful colonial home in Chile to the newlyweds with six months rent paid. The young couple was gone all day: Frías at engineering school and Allende at the Food and Agriculture Organization. One day, thieves broke into the empty

Isabel's brothers, Juan and Francisco, were all smiles on her wedding day.

house and stole food and furniture. Luckily, they did not steal Memé's treasured mirror.

In the Department of Information at the Food and Agriculture Organization, two journalists took Allende under their wing and taught her to write articles. Journalism would turn out to be important to Allende's training as a novelist. A newswriter must grab her audience quickly and keep readers interested until the very end, a necessary skill in writing fiction as well.

Shortly after Allende started writing for the FAO's Department of Information, television stations began broadcasting in Chile. One day, the United Nations was offered fifteen minutes to explain the World Campaign Against Hunger. Ordinarily, Allende's boss would have appeared on the air, but he was ill. Allende had to fill in for him with no advance warning. She did so well that she was offered a weekly spot on television. In her new job, Allende was responsible for all aspects of her program, from the script to the on-air delivery. For fifteen minutes a week, she appeared on television, talking about things that interested her.[8]

Allende wanted to know about everything going on in the world. News, politics, and the community—all fascinated her. Her career as a television journalist was taking off.

In 1963, Allende dreamed she would give birth to a daughter: a "slender child, with dark hair, large black eyes, and a limpid gaze." Her prediction proved to be correct. Shortly after her dream, she learned she was pregnant. On October 22, 1963, Paula was born. Later, in her book *Paula*, Allende would write to her daughter: "Those months you were inside me were a time of perfect happiness."[9]

When Allende returned to work, she felt torn between her job and her desire to be the perfect wife and mother. Sometimes she called in sick so she could spend the day with her baby. During the next year and a half, Allende appeared on television every week. She had become somewhat of a celebrity, and people began to recognize her on the street. Even so, after Allende's husband graduated from engineering school, the young couple was eager for adventure. Allende and Frías both applied for scholarships to study in Europe.

Paula was almost two when the family flew to Geneva, Switzerland. Tío Ramón met them at the airport. The family divided its time between Switzerland, where Allende's parents lived, and Belgium, where they rented a tiny attic apartment above a barbershop. In Belgium, Frías studied engineering, and Allende took a course in television. When classes were not in session, Allende and her husband

Allende, Frías, and their little daughter, Paula, spent part of 1965 and 1966 living in Europe.

Allende and her husband traveled to Europe to study—and explore. When she enrolled in a television class with men from the Congo, Allende had to stifle her outspoken personality in an attempt to bridge the cultural gap.

traveled through Europe in an ancient Volkswagen, camping and carrying Paula in a backpack. When Allende became pregnant in 1966 with their second child, the family decided to return to Chile.

Back home, Allende learned that many people were excited about a wave of political change being talked about in Chile. Her relative, Salvador Allende, was a prominent politician who promised many reforms for poor people. Although a large segment of the population was excited about his ideas, he lost the election to the more conservative candidate.

In many parts of the world, the sixties was a time of rebellion against the old ways of doing things. In the United States, demonstrators marched for civil rights and challenged their country's involvement in the Vietnam War. The feminist movement encouraged women to break free of traditional roles and seek careers. In colleges and universities across America, students protested what they saw as oppressive rules and regulations. A new wave of rock musicians sang about making love not war. Hippies, sometimes called "flower children," experimented with drugs and turned their backs on school and jobs. Allende did not get caught up in the hippie philosophy. Her one concession to the flower children was to paint giant dahlias and sunflowers on the family's house and on her car.

Although Chile's conservative religious patriarchy still held strong, the country was ripe for change. One of these changes would come from women seeking a higher profile in society. The women's movement had arrived, and Allende believed in the cause from the beginning.[10] Her rebellious nature kicked into high gear with the feminist movement. "What I was feeling was like the echo of things that were happening all over the world. Women in Europe, in the United States, were writing, were fighting, were getting organized. . . . I was one of them. I was lucky enough to be born in that generation, and not in my mother's generation," she said.[11]

Nicolás and Paula, ages three and six.

A son, Nicolás, was born in 1966. Frías was working as an engineer on a construction project. The family was happy and secure. Before long, Paula and Nicolás would be running around the garden, climbing trees and pitching tents. Frías's parents lived a block away, on a golf course. They would provide fresh-baked rolls for the children to snack on and an inviting place to play. In the upcoming years, Allende would again juggle motherhood with her journalism career.

5

Feminist and Rebel

In 1967, one of Chile's most socially prominent women decided to start a magazine, called *Paula*. Delia Vergara was a friend of Allende's mother. She had read several of Isabel's letters and was impressed with the young woman's sense of humor. She invited Allende to come to work for her. Vergara was a pioneer in the women's movement, and she wanted to create more than just a fashion magazine. The first issue would be published in August 1967.

Although Allende had no experience as a magazine journalist, she agreed to write a lighthearted column mocking Chile's patriarchal system. Allende launched the column, titled "The Impertinent Ones," by poking fun at different types of Chilean husbands. In later columns, she wrote about controversial issues of the day, including contraception, divorce, abortion, suicide and other subjects rarely discussed in Chile. By using humor, she was able to say things that otherwise would not have been tolerated. Her writing prompted both admiration and scorn from readers.

> *In her magazine column, Allende poked fun at the men of Chile.*

Allende's seven years at *Paula* would contribute greatly to her development as a writer.[1] She also wrote an advice column called "Love Mail" and an astrology section. The astrological forecasts were based on her friends' adventures rather than on any personal psychic knowledge.

One day in 1969, Allende received a call from the morgue in Santiago. A man with the last name of Allende had died. The officials immediately recognized the name and called Isabel Allende to identify the body. She assumed the dead man must be one of her brothers, who had not contacted the family in months. When she arrived at the morgue, she saw that the body was that of a much older man. She said she had never seen this man before in her life. It was not her brother. She called Tío Ramón, who met her at the morgue. He told Isabel that the man was her father.[2]

All these years, Tomás Allende had been living in Santiago. She might have passed him on the street but would not have recognized him. Even as an adult, Isabel was not able to learn why her parents had split up and her father had disappeared. All she knew was that he had strange habits that her mother could not tolerate.

Allende took her usual no-nonsense view of circumstances that might have devastated another person: "I come from a family where no one looks back. We don't have the time for that."[3] Her mother's love kept her from feeling orphaned, she said, and if her father's abandonment affected her at all, it may have been in her rebellion against and distrust of men.[4]

It was through television that Allende expressed her anger against the old ways of doing things. From 1970 to 1975, she hosted two television shows in Santiago. One was an interview program. The other took a poke at Chilean society. Allende herself was living two lives. She filled the role of conservative wife and mother at home, while on television she did a series of what she called "wild things." Allende said these outrageous scenarios were not created to publicize her television program or to attract attention. It was more that she had found an outlet for her feelings of rage and rebelliousness.[5]

Her humorous television program had different names over the years. Two were *Fíjate qu* (Listen Up!) and *La media naranja* (My Better Half). Allende and actress Margara Ureta created scenes, using a candid camera, to prove their point that Chilean men often took a shallow and hypocritical view of women.

For one show, Ureta walked down the street in a pair of old jeans and a blouse. Then she changed into a miniskirt and walked down the same street. When Ureta was wearing the old jeans, the men in the area ignored her. But dressed in a miniskirt, wig, and false eyelashes, she got lots of attention. Allende showed viewers that Chilean men were much more focused on exterior details.[6]

Allende often used this candid-camera format on her show. She became a master at using humor to prove a serious point.

Allende's grandfather slowly adjusted to her notoriety. Tata did not like her long dresses and antique hats. He was not pleased when she painted flowers all over her car. Even more, he disapproved of her feminist philosophy. But because Allende was a good wife, mother,

Feminism

Feminism is the belief that women should be equal to men in all areas of life. Feminists believe that throughout history men have been lauded for their contributions to society while women's contributions have been largely ignored. In the early 1900s women fought for, and gained, the right to vote. Later, in the 1960s, women demanded equal pay for equal work. In the United States, feminist leaders such as Betty Friedan and Gloria Steinem advised women to take action and fight for equality. The National Organization for Women (NOW) took up many feminist causes and achieved many of its goals, such as making it illegal for a company to pay a woman less than a man for the same work.

and housekeeper, he forgave the things that angered him.[7]

In September 1970, Salvador Allende was elected president of Chile. Allende had served as minister of health and had been a senator for many years. He had run for president several times without success. This time, he swept into office under the banner of his Popular Unity coalition.

When Salvador Allende took office, he appointed Isabel's stepfather, Ramón Huidobro, as Chile's ambassador to Argentina. Panchita and Tío Ramón moved to the capital city of Buenos Aires. At this time, many diplomats were being kidnapped, and in 1971 Allende had a dream that Tío Ramón had been kidnapped. Upset by the nightmare, she stayed home from work for two days and wrote a play, called *El Embajador* (*The Ambassador*), about the kidnapping of a diplomat. In the play, as the kidnappers and their hostage spend a year together in a basement, they grow to understand one another. Allende's aunt, an actress, showed an early draft of the play to a theater company, which decided to stage it. Isabel felt embarrassed hearing her dialogue read aloud by the actors. The play clearly needed more work. As she made changes in the script, Allende learned how to make her characters more realistic.[8] The play opened in Santiago in 1972.

By then, Allende had achieved some fame as a journalist and television personality. She was thrilled when Pablo Neruda, the most famous poet in Chile, asked her

Allende's mother, Panchita, with her husband Tomas's cousin Salvador Allende, president of Chile.

Pablo Neruda invited Allende to visit his home.

to visit his seaside home at Isla Negra. Allende planned her interview very carefully. She worked hard to come up with just the right questions to ask the great poet. She also reviewed Neruda's work and read two biographies about his life. She wrote out her list of questions and bought a new tape recorder.

When Allende arrived at Neruda's home, she was fascinated by the strange surroundings. A maze of wood and stone held the poet's collections of seashells, bottles, dolls, books, and paintings. After lunch, she asked if he was ready to be interviewed. Neruda just laughed. She had misunderstood his invitation. He had no intention of being interviewed.

Neruda went on to say that Allende was "the worst" journalist because instead of reporting straight facts, she put her own slant on every story. Not only that, but if there was nothing to report, she made things up. The famous poet told Allende that she should be a novelist instead. The imagination that made her a terrible journalist would make her a terrific storyteller.[9] Years later,

Allende would come to recognize the wisdom of Neruda's advice.

From 1973 to 1974, Allende also wrote for a children's magazine, entitled *Mampato*. When the magazine's director died, Allende filled in as director for a short time. She also published two children's stories and a collection of her humorous magazine columns.

Allende enjoyed her work as a journalist and television

Isabel Allende—journalist, TV personality, and mother of two—would soon find her life turned upside down.

> *The imagination that made Allende a terrible journalist would make her a terrific storyteller.*

personality. She loved the fact that people recognized her on the street. With her blooming confidence, she felt as if she could knock on any door in the city and be invited inside.[10]

Meanwhile, ominous changes had been taking place in the government. These changes would deeply affect Allende and turn her blissful feelings into fear.

6

Flight Into Exile

Chileans who supported President Salvador Allende considered him to be a kind man motivated by high ideals for his country. They believed he was dedicated to helping Chile's poor slum dwellers, miners, and peasants through a socialist form of government. He said he favored change but was determined to keep the country's democratic principles. One of his goals was to free Chile from the foreign corporations that owned many of its profitable natural resources, mainly its copper mines.[1]

Other Chileans, including Isabel Allende's grandfather and his business associates, were horrified when Salvador Allende became president. These businessmen believed Allende's socialist policies would destroy Chile's economy.

In the early seventies, Chileans continued to vote Popular Unity legislators into office. These victories

Socialism

Socialism is the theory that a government should own and manage the producers of food, clothing, and other goods for its country's citizens. Some socialists support class warfare—in which poor citizens overthrow the rich citizens, seize ownership of their wealth, and distribute it to all the people. Other socialists believe in obtaining their goals by peaceful means, such as elections by the people. Socialism has attracted a considerable following in Europe and Latin America. The United States, in contrast, is a capitalist country. The capitalist economic system encourages individuals to own and manage businesses with a minimum of government regulation.

threatened those who believed the government should not interfere in business. The trend also worried foreigners who owned Chilean businesses. In the United States, President Richard Nixon was concerned because the Allende government had taken over American corporations such as the Anaconda and Kennecott copper mines and International Telephone and Telegraph.[2]

The military forces in Chile decided to oust Salvador Allende with a military coup, a takeover of the government by force. The United States supported this decision.

On September 11, 1973, Chilean military forces (the junta) led by General Augusto Pinochet stormed La

Moneda, the presidential palace. Five hours later, Salvador Allende was dead, and the military junta declared itself the new government of Chile. The military junta announced that Allende had committed suicide, though his supporters suspected he had been murdered.

That morning of September 11, Isabel Allende had set out for work as usual, only to find the streets eerily empty. She imagined she had stumbled into one of the science fiction plots she loved as a teenager.[3] It was not until the afternoon that she learned of the military coup and her uncle Salvador's death. The coup would radically change Allende's life. "The first part of my life ended on September 11, 1973," she said.[4]

During the days and weeks following the coup, Popular Unity sympathizers were hauled off to jails, barracks, and concentration camps, where they were imprisoned and tortured. Many people simply disappeared and were never seen or heard from again. So many people disappeared that a new verb was coined to describe the event. It was said that someone "was disappeared" when they vanished without a trace. Many years later, the United Nations interviewed survivors. The resulting 1981 report detailed a variety of tortures used by the military government.

At the magazine *Paula*, Allende and her colleagues were under strict censorship rules established by the military regime. They could publish only what was approved by the military government. Anyone who had

President Salvador Allende, right, named Augusto Pinochet commander of the Chilean army in August 1973. A few weeks later, Pinochet, left, and the army seized control of the country.

been actively involved in Salvador Allende's Popular Unity coalition was fired. Others fled to foreign countries, where they would be safe from Chile's military police. Some of Isabel's colleagues disappeared entirely. She and her co-workers feared their peers had been abducted and murdered. Later, Allende lost both her job as director of the children's magazine *Mampato* and her job at *Paula*. Allende believed she was fired because the military government hated feminism and thought it was as subversive as socialism.[5]

For the next eighteen months, Allende took part in the underground movement in Chile. People who were considered enemies of the state had to go into hiding. Allende helped them find food and shelter, allowed them to stay in her home, and drove them to escape routes out of the country. She did not realize how dangerous her activities were until she was deeply involved in the underground. As the military government tightened its reins of power, helping its enemies became even more perilous. "I knew now that if I was caught, I would be killed or tortured," she said.[6] Later, in her book *My Invented Country*, she described fear as "a permanent metallic taste in my mouth."[7]

Finally, Allende heeded the warnings that it was too dangerous for her to remain in Chile. She learned that Venezuela was home to several thousand Chileans. In 1975, Allende, her husband, and their two children fled to Caracas, Venezuela. Allende's in-laws and her grandfather chose to stay behind in Chile. Allende would never see her beloved Tata again.

Allende's parents also emigrated to Venezuela, moving into the apartment above Isabel's. At first Isabel and her children were terribly homesick for Chile. Unable to find work as a journalist, Allende took a number of jobs simply to earn a paycheck. Her journalism credentials from Chile were ignored because she had no way to prove they were true. In Venezuela, she had to start from scratch. Frías found an engineering job in the interior of the country, seeing his family only on weekends. Isabel stayed in Caracas with Paula and Nicolás. She would write at night, but she ripped up most of her work and threw it away. Exiled from her country, Allende said she felt "like a tree without roots, destined to dry up and die."[8]

In Venezuela, Allende found few opportunities in journalism. She wrote a weekly humor column for the Sunday supplement of the newspaper *El Nacional* that barely paid for the postage to submit the articles. At the age of thirty-five, Allende had lost the celebrity status she had earned in Chile. In Venezuela, she was simply a person like many others, desperately seeking work.

Allende's weekly separation from her husband took its toll on their marriage. In 1978, Allende became involved with another man and moved with him to Spain. Three months later, the affair ended. With no job and no economic resources, she returned to Caracas and her husband. They determined to make their marriage work.

In 1979, Allende was offered a job as an administrator in a school. Colegio Marroco educated primary students in the morning and secondary students in the afternoon. Allende worked both shifts, staying from seven in the morning

Allende lost her celebrity status. In Venezuela, she was simply a person desperately seeking work.

until seven at night. Her duties included keeping the school's accounts. At this point, she firmly believed that women must earn their own money to achieve independence. Without economic freedom, women would remain dependent upon men. Allende worked at the school for four and a half years.

Allende was still working at Colegio Marroco on January 8, 1981, when she began writing the letters that would become her first novel, *The House of the Spirits*. Thinking of the letters as a string of beads, she ended her family saga with the same sentence with which she had begun: "*Barrabás came to us by sea . . .*" She thought that ending the story with the same sentence was like fastening a necklace.[9]

There were so many characters and events in Allende's story that sometimes she confused time periods. When her husband, Miguel Frías, read the manuscript, he sketched a blueprint of the storyline and pinned it

> *Panchita was shocked at first to see her family's secrets laid out in the story.*

on the walls of their dining room. Allende was then able to arrange the events so they unfolded in the right order.[10]

Allende showed the manuscript to her mother, who at first was horrified at the family secrets revealed in the story. Panchita suggested some minor changes and helped Allende choose the title *The House of the Spirits*. With the writing of this first novel, Allende established two habits that have stayed with her: Her mother has served as her first and most demanding critic on every book she has written. And she always begins writing her books on the date January 8, her lucky day.

The women in *The House of the Spirits* demonstrate unique strength of character despite their male-dominated society. When asked if the women characters in the novel are feminists, Allende replied: "All the women in my book are feminists in their fashion; that is, they ask to be free and complete human beings, to be able to fulfill themselves, not to be dependent on men. Each one battles according to her own character and within the possibilities of the epoch in which she happens to be living."[11] Allende dedicated *The House of the Spirits* "to my mother, my grandmother, and all the other extraordinary women of this story." With this book, Allende felt she had finally done something worthwhile with her life.[12]

Miguel Frías celebrated his wife's success along with their entire family. Unfortunately, their happiness was short-lived. Frías's business declined into bankruptcy, and he began suffering fainting spells. A physician told Frías he had diabetes. Then, after a niece began to have similar symptoms, the entire family was tested. The doctors discovered that Frías did not have diabetes. He and the couple's two children, Paula and Nicolás, had inherited a rare metabolic disorder known as porphyria.

> "All the women in my books are feminists in their fashion."

The term *porphyria* is taken from the Greek word *porphyra*—meaning "purple"—because some porphyria patients excrete dark-red urine. Patients with this disorder have an abnormal buildup of porphyrins, a chemical in the body. The symptoms vary and can include sun sensitivity and abdominal pain. At this time, there is no cure for the disease.[13]

The family accepted the news calmly and went on with their lives. Allende had no idea how deeply and profoundly porphyria would affect her in the future.

7

Magical Realist

By 1984, *The House of the Spirits* was a stunning commercial success. The book had been reprinted twelve times in Spanish and had been translated into French, German, Italian, and Norwegian. Readers devoured the thrilling story of the del Valle and Trueba families.

After *The House of the Spirits* was published, Carmen Balcells had told Allende that many people can write a good first novel. The real proof of an author's talents, the literary agent said, is a good second novel.[1] Allende was determined to prove she could do it again.

Of Love and Shadows was published in Spain in 1984. The next year, an English edition of *The House of the Spirits*—translated by Magda Bogin— was published in the United States. It was an immediate hit. *Of Love and Shadows*, too, was published in English (1987) and snapped up by American readers. The English translation was done by Margaret Sayers Peden, who became

Allende's *Of Love and Shadows* had its roots in the abductions that followed the 1973 military coup in Chile.

Allende's regular translator. Allende would continue to write in Spanish, but from that time on, her books would always be published in English as well as in Spanish.

Although Allende's readers loved her stories, the critics did not always agree on their literary merit. Book reviewers for newspapers and magazines praised her work, but some scholars claimed it was superficial and unoriginal. They accused her of imitating another famous Latin American writer, Gabriel García Márquez, who also used magic realism in his stories.[2] Still, these criticisms had little if any impact on the millions of readers who continued to buy Allende's novels.

Allende had written *Of Love and Shadows* in response to some grisly news from her homeland. In 1978, newspapers reported that the bodies of fifteen men were discovered in an abandoned mine shaft in Chile. The corpses were *desaparecidos* (the disappeared ones) murdered during the military coup of 1973.[3]

Allende imagined the women who must have searched and searched for their husbands, sons, and fathers, and all the while they were at the bottom of the mine shaft. She could not stop thinking about the women. For Allende, the terrible discovery symbolized all who had been abducted and murdered in Chile and throughout Latin America. She began collecting news clippings about the gruesome case and determined to write a story about it.[4]

Of Love and Shadows describes a Latin American

Even thirty years later, in 2003, relatives of "the disappeared ones" held a vigil in memory of their loved ones.

country in the grip of a brutal military dictatorship. Despite the violence in the book, Allende considers it a story about love and about unity among people.[5] Most of the reviews for the book were positive. One newspaper critic called Allende's writing "so warm, so human, so filled with love for her characters and her country, that in the end human nature . . . counteracts the horror and casts light and love where before there was only shadow." Another critic noted Allende's "profound political awareness" and called her "a born storyteller."[6]

> *Allende imagined the women who must have searched and searched for their husbands, sons, and fathers.*

Still, some critics insisted the book was too political or too sentimental. Allende responded that they had trouble accepting her belief that love is stronger than hatred.[7]

Allende continued to write letters to her mother every day. Tío Ramón had turned seventy, and he and Panchita had decided to go back to Chile. Allende was not yet ready to return to her homeland.

Allende's literary success put her in great demand as a lecturer and creative writing teacher. During these years, she traveled to the United States to become a visiting professor at various colleges: Montclair State College in New Jersey in the spring of 1985; the University of Virginia in the spring of 1988; Barnard College in New York City in fall 1988; and the University of California at Berkeley in spring 1989. Her books were becoming the subject of literary analysis by academics, who wrote essays about the structure of her novels and the characters. They came up with all kinds of themes that Allende herself had never imagined when she was writing her books. Allende believes every aspect of life contains mystery, including writing. She has said most writers cannot explain what they do, and if they are pressured to give an explanation, they will fall apart.[8]

Allende also began to receive awards for her writing—both literary honors and recognition of her popularity among readers. She has acknowledged the attention with a down-to-earth attitude: "I never expected that the weird craft of writing would be of any interest to the general public, nor that a writer could become a sort of celebrity and be expected to behave like one."[9]

With two successful novels, Allende could finally believe in herself as an author. When she began her third novel, she was ready to pursue a full-time literary career.

Allende's personal life was not going as well. In 1987, after twenty-five years of marriage, she and Miguel Frías divorced. Allende was forty-four years old. The children, Paula and Nicolás, were young adults. Allende and Frías treated each other with courtesy and respect during the divorce and would remain lifelong friends.

That year, Allende's third book, *Eva Luna*, was published in both Spain and the United States, with the English translation done by Margaret Sayers Peden. In *Eva Luna*, Allende the storyteller created a storyteller as her heroine. The book opens with Eva introducing herself to the reader: "My name is Eva, which means 'life,' according to a book of names my mother consulted." Allende quickly draws the reader into Eva's fantastic and amazing tales. Many reviewers praised the book with words such as *wonderful, elegant, exotic, sumptuous,* and *magnificent*.

Allende has said that each book she writes is triggered

Margaret Sayers Peden has translated many of Allende's books. She is one of the world's top translators.

by a different passion or emotion. About *Eva Luna*, she said, "*Eva Luna* had a wonderful, positive feeling. That was the discovery that finally I liked being a woman; for forty years I wanted to be a man; I thought that it was much better to be a man. When I was in my forties, I discovered that I had done all the things that men do and many more, that I had succeeded in my life. I was okay. And that's what the story is about; it's about storytelling and about being a woman."[10]

After her divorce, Allende imagined that she would spend the rest of her days alone and devoted to her work.[11] But as in her stories, the unexpected happened. San Francisco lawyer William Gordon attended a lecture Allende gave in San Jose, California. Afterward, a group from the lecture went to dinner at an Italian restaurant. Gordon had read *Of Love and Shadows* and wanted to meet the author of such a deeply romantic story. Allende found herself drawn to the handsome American lawyer who spoke fluent Spanish.

After their first date in San Francisco, Gordon drove Allende to the airport. She shocked him by asking him if he were in love with her. "Poor guy, he almost drove off the road. He had to pull over, and he said, 'What are you talking about? We just met.'"[12]

Undaunted, Allende drafted what she called a contract and sent it to Gordon. It said that she would give their relationship a try in the United States, but she had two major requirements. First, he must date only her. Second, he must allow her to redecorate his house. He agreed to both, and in December 1987, Allende moved from Venezuela to San Rafael, California, to be with him. They were married on July 17, 1988. Allende was now a United States resident.

Meanwhile, in Allende's homeland of Chile, political change was taking place. In 1988, the military dictator General Pinochet agreed to allow Chileans to hold a plebiscite, or vote. The question was whether or not they wanted him to stay in the presidency. If they voted no, a

Allende's romance with William Gordon was unpredictable and unconventional—like some of her novels.

democratic election for president would be held the following year. Allende was determined to vote against Pinochet in the plebiscite.[13] It could lead to the end of General Pinochet's reign of terror.

Allende returned to Chile for the first time in thirteen years. To her surprise, when she and Gordon arrived at the airport in Santiago, a small crowd waited to greet them. Many fans brought copies of *The House of the Spirits* for Allende to sign. Allende felt ecstatic to be in her homeland again. She was thrilled that the majority of Chileans voted against Pinochet in the plebiscite. A year later, Allende would go back to Chile to help vote Pinochet out of office in the general election.[14] In 1990, democracy would be restored to Chile.

Back in the United States, while Allende was teaching creative writing at the University of California at Berkeley, she received the Library Journal's Best Book Award and the Before Columbus Foundation Award. Also in 1989, *The Stories of Eva Luna* was published. Eva, her character from *Eva Luna*, narrated this collection of stories. Allende said each story was sparked by a different event or emotion: "By something that I had read in the news. By a story someone told me that stayed with

Democracy

Democracy is a system of government in which the citizens control how the government is run. The word *democracy* comes from two Greek words: *demos*, meaning "the people" and *kratia*, meaning "to rule." Using their votes, citizens elect their leaders. Once they are in office, the leaders are regulated by laws that define their power. Civil liberties such as freedom of speech and the press, the right to choose one's friends and associates, and freedom of religion are also part of a democratic government.

me for a long time and in a way grew inside me. And then one day, it was ready to be written."[15]

For Allende, the most meaningful story in the collection is "And Of Clay Are We Created." It is based on a horrifying event that occurred in Colombia, South America, in 1985. The volcano Nevado del Ruiz erupted, producing a mud slide that buried a village beneath it. Thirteen-year-old Omaira Sánchez became trapped in the mud and debris. Rescuers were unable to dig her out. Omaira was imprisoned there on the side of the mountain for three days before she died. News media witnessed this terrible event. Allende was haunted by Omaira's eyes as she looked out from the mud that trapped her. For years afterward, Allende kept a photograph of Omaira on her desk.[16] Eventually, she understood why the girl became so important to her. The story took on deeper meaning as tragic events unfolded in Allende's own life.

8

The Writer's Journey

On December 6, 1991, while Allende was in Barcelona, Spain, for the publication of her latest novel, *The Infinite Plan*, her daughter, Paula, was rushed to the hospital in Madrid. Paula and her husband, Ernesto, lived in Spain. At the hospital, when Paula had complications due to her porphyria, she was not given the proper medication. Her brain was severely damaged. With her mother at her side, Paula slipped into a coma.[1]

The next six months were agonizing ones for Allende as she sat by her daughter's bedside in the hospital in Madrid. Allende's mother joined her during much of her vigil, as did Paula's heartbroken young husband. Gordon traveled to Spain to be with Allende when he could.

Allende began to write a long letter to Paula as she lay in the coma. It begins, "Listen, Paula. I am going to

Just a few months after this 1991 picture, Paula lapsed into a coma.

tell you a story, so that when you wake up you will not feel so lost."[2]

"I wrote *Paula* without knowing that it would become a book," said Allende. "It was the journal I kept as I sat in the dark corridors of the Madrid hospital, trying to ward off the specter of death."[3]

The doctors could not revive Paula from her coma. The best that could be managed was that Paula was finally able to breathe on her own. As soon as Paula could breathe without the help of a machine, Allende brought her home to the United States. There, she consulted one doctor after another, but no one was able to help her daughter.

Writing her letter to Paula helped Allende cope with the ordeal of watching and waiting as hope ebbed away. Describing her pain helped her feel less overwhelmed by sorrow.[4] Only then did Allende realize the significance of the suffering young girl whose picture she had kept on her desk. "When Paula fell into a coma . . . I remembered the face of Omaira Sánchez. My daughter was trapped in her body, as the girl had been trapped in mud. Only then did I understand why I had thought about her all those years, and finally could decipher the message in those intense black eyes: patience, courage, resignation, dignity in the face of death."[5]

One night, Paula appeared to Allende in a dream. Paula wore her nightgown and rabbit fur slippers and sat at Allende's feet in her bed. Paula told her mother she wanted to be free to die and follow the radiant path

> **"I wrote Paula without knowing that it would become a book."**

before her.[6] The dream helped Allende understand that she must stop clinging so desperately to her daughter.

Paula died on December 6, 1992, exactly one year after she had become ill. As Paula lay dying, Allende felt the presence of all those spirits who had gone on before her. Surrounded by her family, Paula died in her mother's arms.[7]

Allende always began her books on the same date: January 8. But the January after Paula died, Allende was suffering such grief that it was impossible to begin another book. Then she realized the book was right there in the pages of the journal she had written at her daughter's bedside. It was *Paula*.[8]

Every day as Allende worked to make her journal into a book, tears overcame her. Her assistant told her to stop writing, because it was obviously too painful. But Allende refused, saying the writing helped her contain and control the pain.

Allende believed that experiencing her daughter's illness and death made her a stronger person. "I have a feeling now that I can face pain in a better way," she said.[9] The experience also confirmed Allende's belief that love is the highest value. "What I learned from so much suffering was that all that is left at the end is the love that you give. Not even the love that you receive, because Paula could not give me anything. She only received. But I was left with the everlasting treasure of the love that I gave her."[10]

Nature's beauty was a refuge for Allende as she grieved for her daughter. San Rafael, California, where she now lived, made her think of her beloved homeland. California's rough coastline, hills, foliage, birds, and even the cloud formations, reminded her of Chile.[11] Allende also enjoyed California's Hispanic culture. She had come to think of the state as her home.[12] In 1993, Allende became a United States citizen.

For Allende, starting each new book on January 8 of a new year is not her only tradition. Most writers have what they refer to as their process of creating a book, and Allende is no exception. She writes until the first draft is finished. During this time, she does not socialize: "I'm just locked away, writing."[13]

She allows the first sentence of the book to come from intuition, not from reason. "When I wrote the first sentence of *The House of the Spirits*, which is 'Barrabás came to us by sea,' I didn't yet know who Barrabás was or why he had come. The book ends with the same sentence. It's something magical that I can't explain."[14]

Even though she is fluent in English, Allende always writes in her native Spanish, to be translated later into English. Allende burns a candle as she works. The lighted candle is a symbol of her belief that the story already exists. "Fiction is something that happens to me in spite of myself. It happens in my belly, not in my mind."[15] As the storyteller, it is her job to illumine the story and bring it to life for her readers. She also lights the candle because she does not like clocks. She writes for as long as the candle burns. Then she can take time off to have dinner and socialize in the evenings.

Once Allende has completed three drafts of her novel, she sends the manuscript to her mother in Chile. Her mother is her harshest and smartest critic, and Allende trusts Panchita's judgment completely. She follows all the editing suggestions her mother marks on the manuscript with her red pencil. Allende believes the changes will result in a better book.[16] After those changes are made, the book goes directly to the publisher.

California's Hispanic Culture

The state of California has its roots in Hispanic culture. Spanish sailors first explored the coast in 1542. In San Diego in 1769, Father Junipero Serra established the first of many missions that have become popular tourist attractions in California. Mexican settlers traveled to California on El Camino Real (The King's Highway—now called Highway 101) in the 1800s.

Today, Hispanic culture thrives in California. Every year on Cinco de Mayo (the Fifth of May), festivities commemorate Mexico's victory after the French invaded in 1862. Throughout California, Cinco de Mayo parties and parades celebrate freedom and liberty.

Allende and her son, Nicolás. Writing and family helped Allende cope with Paula's death.

The Infinite Plan, published in English in 1993, is Allende's first novel set in the United States. Based on the life of her husband, William Gordon, it is the story of a fictional character, Gregory Reeves, and his family. Gregory is the son of a preacher who claims life is controlled by an "infinite plan." When the preacher becomes critically ill, the family moves into the Los Angeles barrio to live with a Mexican family. Poverty and violence stalk the young Gregory. As an adult, Gregory lives a self-destructive lifestyle and eventually concludes,

Allende, her husband, and her agent, Carmen Balcells.

"There is no infinite plan. Just the strife of living." Finally, Gregory realizes that the only quest worth following is the quest for his soul.

Many critics noted with displeasure that in *The Infinite Plan*, Allende departed from the magic realism of *The House of the Spirits*. There were other complaints, too. Robert Bly, a critic for the *New York Times Book Review*, said that *The Infinite Plan* was not as enjoyable as *The House of the Spirits*, but that it was more ambitious and idealistic.[17]

Kathryn Hughes of *New Statesman & Society* found the book to be mundane and boring, with "description at the expense of dialogue to produce page-long paragraphs of unrelieved tedium."[18]

In *The Christian Science Monitor*, Merle Rubin said that although Allende's writing was "merely competent" the book was "a large canvas, filled with characters, action, and historical scenery."[19]

> **Allende believes that she and other women writers have a special gift to give to the world.**

The Infinite Plan may have been criticized by reviewers and scholars—but Allende's readers did not seem to care. Her fans throughout the world bought and read the book with pleasure.

9

The Most
Generous Thing

In January 1994, Allende was present at the birth of her third grandchild. The baby, born to her son Nicolás and his wife, Celia, came into the world in the same room in which Paula had spent her final hours. Though she would always miss Paula, Allende had a rich, full life with her husband and their children and grandchildren. Her writing career continued to bring her many rewards.

Nearly ten years after the novel *The House of the Spirits* was published in the United States, a movie version opened in U.S. theaters. Meryl Streep and Jeremy Irons starred as Clara and Esteban Trueba, Allende's fictional grandparents. Vanessa Redgrave, Winona Ryder, and Antonio Banderas were also featured. Movie critic Janet Maslin of *The New York Times* raved about the film, saying it was filled with "understated miracles."[1]

At first, Allende was surprised at the actors chosen

for the movie, because many of them were tall and blond. But once she saw the movie, she was charmed by it. Allende was impressed with the actors' ability to bring her story to life. "My grandmother was a little woman with dark eyes, small as a dwarf. She appears in the film in the person of Meryl Streep as tall, blond, and with blue eyes. And yet it felt to me, as I watched the film, that Meryl Streep was my grandmother."[2]

Allende had a continuing sense that Memé was with her. "When I say she has been with me it's true, not in

Could tall, blond Meryl Streep, right, and Vanessa Redgrave, left, play Allende's small, dark relatives?

the sense that she appears like a ghost, floating and moving chains around, no. But every time that I'm at a crossroads and I'm lost and confused, I think what would she do. . . . When I'm really frightened, I ask for protection and I feel that she has protected me. She has saved me from situations I have put myself in that were pretty risky."[3]

The world premier of the movie *Of Love and Shadows* also took place in 1994. The film starred Antonio Banderas and Jennifer Connelly. Allende was glad a

Antonio Banderas and other famous Hollywood actors have starred in movie versions of Allende's novels.

woman, Betty Kaplan, directed the movie. Although *Of Love and Shadows* was a thriller, Allende said that Kaplan kept the beauty and romance of the book.

The book *Paula* was published in Spanish in 1994, and in English in 1995. The book describes Allende's experiences while Paula lay in the coma, but also weaves in personal family stories to create a memoir. She relates events that happened to her, Isabel, throughout her life up until the time Paula fell into the coma and died. Many critics hailed the book as another great success for Allende.

Some dissenting critics have pointed out that there is more in the book about Isabel than there is about Paula. They even suggested that maybe the book should have been called *Isabel*. In response, others have pointed out that Allende's vivid storytelling highlights Paula's quietness as she lies in the coma. The writing shows the contrast in personalities between mother and daughter. Allende is prone to flights of imagination, while Paula lived her life in a mature and simple way.[4] Either way, there is no doubt that the book honors Paula and is a lasting tribute to the love between mother and daughter.

Paula became a bestseller both in Europe and in the United States. Allende was pleased by the book's reception, but she wanted to do even more to honor her daughter's memory. She decided to use money earned from sales of the book to create a charitable foundation in Paula's honor.[5]

The Isabel Allende Foundation was established on

As a tribute to her daughter's commitment to helping others, Allende donates money earned by the book *Paula* to her foundation.

December 9, 1996, to help people in need, especially women and children. Paula had volunteered as an educator and psychologist in poor communities in Venezuela and Spain. "When in doubt," said her mother, "[Paula's] motto was: 'What is the most generous thing to do?'" Allende created the foundation to honor her daughter's "life work, her ideals, and her compassion."[6]

The foundation helps charities provide financial aid for education, health care, and other services for women and children in need. Tom Wilson, executive director of the Canal Community Alliance in Allende's hometown of San Rafael, called Allende an "angel" for all she has done to help women and children. He believes Allende's generous financial contributions have helped save lives.[7]

The city of Los Angeles named Allende Author of the Year in 1996 and set aside January 16, 1996, as Isabel Allende Day.

In 1997, after the success of *Paula*, Allende had writer's block. She felt as if her stories had dried up. One night she dreamed of four Indians emerging from the heart of South America. The Indians carried a large box. As they carried the box across jungles, rivers, mountains, and villages, the box absorbed every sound. The world became quiet. All sounds were swallowed up by the box. Allende awoke believing she must go to South America to search for the box. A year later, she took a trip to the Amazon jungle in Brazil. There, the vast green world filled with exotic plants and animals restored the inspiration she needed to tell her stories.[8]

In 1998, Allende won two prestigious awards in the United States. The Dorothy and Lillian Gish Prize, one of the largest prizes in the arts, brought her a silver medallion and a cash award of $200,000. The prize is given annually by the Dorothy and

> *In 1997, after the success of Paula, Allende had writer's block. She felt as if her stories had dried up.*

Lillian Gish Prize Trust. It honors an outstanding contribution to beauty and to our "enjoyment and understanding of life."[9]

The actress Lillian Gish wanted to reward those people who had made special contributions to society. She wanted to encourage other people to follow their examples in doing good. Allende was the fifth recipient of the award. Other recipients have included the singer/songwriter Bob Dylan, artist/director Robert Wilson, film director Ingmar Bergman, and architect Frank Gehry.

Allende also won the Sara Lee Frontrunner Award, given to those who demonstrate continuous commitment to their work and who motivate others to do the same.[10]

Exotic travels have been part of Allende's life since childhood. She and her friend Tabra, right, visited India in 1995.

Allende is open to taking risks and seeking new challenges as an artist. *Aphrodite: A Memoir of the Senses*, published in English in 1998, was very different from her novels and from her memoir about Paula. *Aphrodite* is a combination cookbook and memoir. Allende compares the themes of food and romance. Her mother contributed all the recipes. Allende has said that writing the lighthearted *Aphrodite* helped her come out

Lori Barra, who designed Allende's book *Aphrodite*, married the author's son, Nicolás.

of her period of mourning for Paula.[11] The book was considered delightful by many critics.

In 1999, Allende's sixth work of fiction, *Daughter of Fortune*, was published in both Spanish and English. This historical saga takes place in Chile and California during the California Gold Rush of 1849. Allende creates one of her typically strong heroines in Eliza Sommers. When Eliza becomes pregnant at sixteen, she defies the rules and customs of her time by running away to find her boyfriend. Trailing him from Chile to the California Gold Rush, she enters into a quest filled with danger and hardships. Along the way, she meets Tao Chi'en, a Chinese doctor who saves her life and becomes her closest friend and ally. *Daughter of Fortune* is about freedom, which Allende has called a recurrent theme in her own life.[12]

A *Time* magazine reviewer, R. Z. Sheppard, wrote that Eliza Sommers "runs circles around everyone else" in the novel. He called *Daughter of Fortune* a "rip-roaring girls' adventure story" and said the book is part of the new feminist approach in literature in which girls from past generations act out contemporary values. Sheppard said that Allende writes from a woman's point of view with confidence and control and that she writes about romance as a fact of life.[13]

Michiko Kakutani, writing for *The New York Times*, was not as complimentary, calling the book "a bodice-ripper romance."[14]

Daughter of Fortune is what is known as a hero quest. Many books and movies feature a hero or heroine who desires a goal and goes on a perilous journey to obtain that goal. The journey may be an inner one of the heart and soul. It may also be an outer journey through dangerous territory. Allende often writes about heroes and heroines who face inner and outer obstacles yet overcome them, as she herself has done during her lifetime.

Allende's heroines often rebel against the belief that men should rule over women. Her stories show women taking charge of their lives and solving their problems.

Rather than preach about feminism, her books excite readers with their independent heroines.

On February 17, 2000, Oprah Winfrey chose *Daughter of Fortune* to be her thirtieth book club pick. Allende was the first Hispanic author to be chosen by Oprah.[15] In 2001, Allende appeared on *The Oprah Winfrey Show* as a guest author. The talk show host had many questions about Paula's illness. Allende answered them all in her gracious and open fashion, charming Oprah and her audience.

Daughter of Fortune was already a bestseller, but after being chosen for Oprah's Book Club, sales shot even

The Hero Quest

"There are only two or three human stories, and they go on repeating themselves," said author Willa Cather.[16] Many writers would agree. A majority of stories share the same basic elements, whether they are fairy tales, literary novels, or Hollywood thrillers. A hero or heroine must take a journey. The heroic character must leave comfortable surroundings and venture into the unknown. On this journey, the hero will be tested and will have to overcome obstacles to obtain a goal. Finally, the hero will win the prize and return home. Readers cheer for a hero who overcomes hardship to accomplish a difficult goal.

higher. Isabel Allende had become one of the most widely read living woman authors in the world.

Allende is the first Latin American woman to enter publishing on such a grand scale. Like the heroines of her novels, Allende struck out on her own and fought hard to earn her independence.

Mystery and Memory

In 2001, Allende's novel *Portrait in Sepia* was published. Featuring some of the characters from *The House of the Spirits* and *Daughter of Fortune*, it is the third book in the trilogy involving the del Valle family. Its young heroine is Aurora del Valle, who is haunted by nightmares and cannot remember the first five years of her life. A photographer, she uses her own artistry as well as family photograph albums to solve the mystery of her early years. In the process, she matures as an artist and a woman. She also becomes the memory keeper for the family.

Aurora introduces herself in the first chapter of *Portrait in Sepia*, confiding to the reader: "There are so many secrets in my family that I may never have time to unveil them all."[1]

Allende herself knows what it is like to live in a secretive family, and recording memories is an ongoing theme in her books. Solving the mysteries of memory and searching for her own identity have been lifelong quests for the author.[2] Allende is quick to point out that no one's memory is 100 percent reliable: "If you and I witness the same event, we will recall it and recount it differently."[3]

Always a wanderer, Allende finds her roots in memory. She believes that memory and imagination are so closely intertwined that they cannot be separated: "If we were to remember without imagination, we would use no adjectives. It would be just nouns. But in life we remember the color, the flavor, the emotion. Not the facts."[4]

Andrew Ervin reviewed *Portrait in Sepia* in *The New York Times*, saying, "Isabel Allende makes it look easy."[5] The writing may look easy, but it is hard work. In fiction writing, an author must present characters that make the reader care about them. Allende does this by creating complex characters that are fascinating, not perfect. Allende's characters seem like real people to the reader because of their combination of strengths and weaknesses.

Aurora's grandmother, Paulina del Valle, is an example of a complex character. Bossy and sharp-tongued, she rules the family by manipulating them to get her own way. Yet her intelligence and sense of humor make up for her unlikable traits. When Paulina finds out that Aurora's mother has died in childbirth, she attempts to steal the baby. Readers may not like Paulina, but they will most likely have strong feelings about her plotting

Allende says memory and imagination are so closely interwoven that they cannot be separated.

to take control of her new baby granddaughter. And most readers will be eager to find out what Paulina does next. Fascinating characters keep readers immersed in the writer's imaginary world. Allende is a master of creating character.

Now a grandmother herself, Allende loves telling stories to her three grandchildren. They asked her to write a story for them, and she decided to grant their request and write a novel for young people. Allende says she created the story using research and imagination. This time the hero would be fifteen-year-old Alexander Cold. The book is an adventure story, but it is also about a boy growing up and getting to know himself.

City of the Beasts, aimed at ages ten and up, was published in 2002 and is the first book in Allende's trilogy for young people. The story opens when Alex's mother is seriously ill. Alex is sent to live temporarily with his grandmother, Kate Cold, a journalist. Far from being a cuddly grandmother, Kate seems to delight in making Alex's life miserable. Once, for his birthday, she sent him a box of chocolates injected with hot-pepper sauce.

Kate whisks Alex off to the Amazon, where they join an expedition to find a nine-foot-tall beast rumored to be killing people in the jungle. Their group includes an archaeologist, a doctor, two photographers, a rich businessman, and their guide. The guide's daughter, Nadia Santos, becomes Alex's companion in a flight of fantastic adventures in which they are kidnapped by a lost

Indian tribe and then eventually find the ferocious beast.

Allende could draw from her own past to understand how Alex Cold felt in new and dangerous territory. As a girl whisked off to Patagonia by her grandfather, she had experienced exciting adventures in awe-inspiring surroundings.

Several reviewers noted that partway through *City of the Beasts*, Allende returns to the magic realism of her first novels. Many reviews were critical of the book. Nora Krug of *The New York Times* wrote that although the book opens with a bang, there are too many stories going on in the plot. She also complained that the book has shallow characters and unrealistic events.[6]

Jane P. Fenn, in her review for *School Library Journal*, was more positive. She liked the mysticism and fantastic happenings in the book and thought it would appeal to teens interested in the rain forest.[7]

Allende created many exciting adventures in *City of the Beasts*. Toward the end of the book, Alex crawls down a narrow tunnel, deep into the core of the earth. There, he has been told, he will find the healing waters to cure his mother's disease. The reader is pulled along by the suspense. Will Alex find the water and return safely?

Allende's young grandson Alejandro sparked the idea for her next book. She was looking in the mirror one day, counting her wrinkles, when Alejandro slapped her on the back and informed her that she was not so old. She would live at least three more years, he assured her. His comment made her laugh, but it also made her think about where she wanted to live the rest of her life.

Although she considered herself an American, Allende missed her native Chile. She decided to write a book of her memories of her homeland. *My Invented Country* was published in 2003.

The library journal *Kirkus Reviews* compared *My Invented Country* to a kaleidoscope because of the colorful mix of images of Chile.[8] *My Invented Country* is not a chronological list of memories, nor is it a dry history of the country. Allende's emotions guided her writing. One of those emotions is her feeling that Chile is better than anyplace else in the world. "The first time I visited San Francisco, and there before my eyes were those gentle golden hills, the majesty of forests, and the green mirror of the bay, my only comment was that it looked a lot like the coast of Chile."[9]

For Allende, the history of her country is also the history of her family. In *My Invented Country*, she again tells stories about her relatives: her grandmother with psychic powers; her grandfather the patriarch; her mother and stepfather, the diplomats; and her beloved children, Paula and Nicolás.

Both Chile and the United States have been favorite settings in Allende's novels. These two countries have stirred her loyalty and affection. Finally, Allende discovered that she did not have to choose between Chile and the United States. She realized, "I can have both. And I can be totally bicultural. And I can get the best of both cultures, and use both."[10]

Kingdom of the Golden Dragon, Allende's second young adult novel, came out in English to mixed reviews in 2004. *Dragon* also features Alex Cold, his friend Nadia, and his grandmother Kate. This time, the three journey to the Himalayas. There, they are confronted with corporate villains intent on kidnapping the peaceful society's king and stealing a golden dragon from the kingdom.

Kirkus Reviews called Allende's writing in *Dragon* "clunky" and "awkward."[11] In *Booklist*, reviewer Hazel Rochman said that although the Himalayan setting is

Allende's books are as varied and adventurous as her life.

thrilling, the book is too much like a travelogue. The second half of the book picks up the pace.[12] *Publisher's Weekly* rhapsodized about the book, writing that "the mystic aura that surrounds the story [adds] depth and excitement to a classic battle of good versus evil."[13]

Every reader brings his or her own beliefs and experiences to a story. Therefore, readers often have entirely different opinions of the same story. Allende, like all famous writers, has learned to live with the differing views of the critics and stay true to her own voice.

In the third book in the trilogy, *Forest of the Pygmies* (2005), Allende sends Alexander Cold and his grandmother to Africa, where they go on a safari and discover a society of pygmies. In *Zorro: A Novel* (2005), pirate adventures and folk stories are interlaced with Spanish history and California history to reinvent the legendary Zorro—elegant aristocrat by day, swashbuckling hero by night.

After many years in the United States, Allende feels at home. She became an American citizen in 1993, but it was not until September 11, 2001, that she became an American in her heart. On that day, terrorists hijacked jet planes and crashed them into the World Trade Center towers in New York City, the Pentagon in Washington, D.C., and a field in Pennsylvania. Isabel Allende mourned with all Americans at the devastation and loss of life.

Exactly twenty-eight years earlier, on September 11, 1973, the military coup had overthrown the government of Chile, leaving Salvadore Allende dead. In 1973, Isabel Allende felt as if she had lost her country of Chile. In 2001, through the tragedy shared with other Americans, she felt as if she gained a country in the United States.[14]

Isabel Allende and William Gordon built their dream house on a hill overlooking the San Francisco Bay. They named it *La Casa de los Espíritus*, which is Spanish for *The House of the Spirits*. They are surrounded by friends and family. Nicolás and his family live nearby and are

On September 11, 1973, Isabel lost her uncle Salvador and her homeland of Chile. On September 11, 2001, she realized that she had built a new life, embracing her destiny in the United States.

Becoming a U.S. Citizen

If you were not born in the United States, you may still become a U.S. citizen. First you must be a legal permanent resident for five years, or three years if you are married to a U.S. citizen. You must be eighteen years or older and have lived for at least three months in the state in which you are applying for citizenship. Becoming a citizen also involves some study. You must pass a test that shows you can speak and write in English. Another test questions basic knowledge of United States history and government. Then you must take an oath of allegiance to the United States and renounce loyalty to your native country.

frequent visitors at the villa. "I have adapted to the rhythm of this extraordinary place," Allende writes of her home in California. "I have favorite spots where I spend time leafing through books and walking and talking with friends; I like my routines, the seasons of the years, the huge oaks around my house, the scent of my cup of tea . . . the siren that warns ships of fog in the bay."[15]

Allende and Gordon love to entertain. One of their dinner parties was featured in the magazine *Coastal Living*, with photographs of their guests enjoying a gourmet meal on the patio. Allende loves flowers and is pictured surrounded by bright daisies, mums, and lilies. Her flowing black lace dress complements her dark eyes. Her animated features appear to crackle with energy as she converses with a guest. Bright reds, blues and yellows adorn the food, the flowers, and the accessories, reminding the reader of Allende's colorful life and personality.

Isabel Allende has had a long and distinguished career. She has received more than fifty awards and has been given honorary degrees from a number of universities. She has traveled all over the world as a lecturer and professor of literature. She is one of the most popular writers in the world, with her books translated into thirty languages and more than 10 million copies sold worldwide. The Isabel Allende Foundation helps people in need in her community and around the world.

Allende's life has been filled with obstacles: abandonment by her father, exile from her beloved homeland, the tragic death of her daughter, Paula. No matter what has happened in her life, she writes consistently. When Paula lay in a coma, writing helped Allende cope with her pain.

Allende has devoted her life to her passion for writing: "I write to communicate, to survive, to make the world more understandable. . . . I write because if I didn't I would die."[16] In writing, Allende has found her true home. "Nothing makes my soul sing more than writing," she says. "It makes me feel young, strong, powerful, happy. Wow!"[17]

> "Nothing makes my soul sing more than writing. It makes me feel young, strong, powerful, happy. Wow!"

Allende has worked hard to earn her reputation as a celebrated author. Her career has been almost as fantastic as her magical stories. And yet she believes that her most significant achievement is not her writing but the love she shares with her family.[18] When asked to explain her greatest achievement, she replied, "Motherhood." She says the success of her books is not important in the larger scheme of things. Someday, people may not read or remember her. Her love for her children and grandchildren is the most important thing in her life. Love for family is who she is as a person.[19]

Throughout her long career, Allende has always insisted that love, and understanding among all people, are her highest values. Despite the world's problems, she has hope for the future. Isabel Allende, through her words and her life, shares that hope with readers all over the world.

Chronology

1942—Born on August 2, in Lima, Peru.

1945—When her parents' marriage ends, Isabel moves with her mother and siblings to their grandparents' home in Santiago, Chile.

1952—Mother remarries and family moves to La Paz, Bolivia.

1955—Family moves to Beirut, Lebanon.

1958—Returns home to Santiago, Chile; meets engineering student Miguel Frías.

1959—Receives high school diploma.

1959 –1965—Works for Food and Agriculture Organization of the United Nations in Santiago.

1962—Marries Miguel Frías; produces a weekly television show.

1963—Birth of daughter, Paula.

1964—With husband and baby, travels and lives in Europe.

1966—Birth of son, Nicolás, in Chile.

1967—Begins career as journalist at the magazine *Paula*.

1970—Hosts and produces two television shows, a humor program and an interview show; Salvador Allende is elected president of Chile.

1971—Writes a play, *The Ambassador*.

1972—Play is performed in Santiago.

1973—Military coup takes control of Chilean government and Salvador Allende dies; civil liberties are suspended by the military junta.

1974—Assists victims of political persecution.

1975—Family leaves Chile and goes into exile in Caracas, Venezuela.

1979—Works as school administrator in Caracas.

1981—Begins writing her first novel, *The House of the Spirits*.

1983—*The House of the Spirits* is named best novel of the year in Chile.

1984—Allende is named author of the year in Germany; second novel, *Of Love and Shadows*, is published in Spain; a short story for children, "La gorda de porcelana" ("The Porcelain Fat Lady"), is published in Spain.

1985—*The House of the Spirits* is published in the United States.

1987—Is divorced from Miguel Frías; *Eva Luna* is published in Spain.

1988—Marries William Gordon on July 17 in San Francisco; moves to San Rafael, California.

1989—Allende is a visiting professor in Creative Writing at the University of California, Berkeley, and the University of Virginia, Charlottesville.

1990—Returns to Chile for the first time in fifteen years.

1991—Daughter Paula is hospitalized in Spain, suffers brain damage, and lapses into a coma.

1992—Paula dies at Allende's home in California.

1993—Allende becomes a U.S. citizen; *The Infinite Plan* is published in the United States.

1994—*The House of the Spirits* premieres in U.S. movie theaters; Allende receives honorary doctorate at Bates College in Maine; *Of Love and Shadows* is produced as a movie, starring Antonio Banderas.

1995—*Paula* is published in the United States.

1996—Isabel Allende Foundation is established in honor of Paula.

1998—Wins Dorothy and Lillian Gish Prize and Sara Lee Frontrunner Award; *Aphrodite: A Memoir of the Senses* is published.

1999—*Daughter of Fortune* is published; Allende travels to promote the book.

2000—*Daughter of Fortune* is selected by Oprah's Book Club; it is the first Oprah pick written by a Hispanic author.

2001—*Portrait in Sepia* is published.

2002—Allende receives Excellence in International Literature and Arts Award; first young adult novel, *City of the Beasts,* is published.

2003—*My Invented Country* is published.

2004—Allende is named to the American Academy of Arts and Letters; *Kingdom of the Golden Dragon* is published.

2005—*Zorro: A Novel* and *Forest of the Pygmies* are published.

Books by
Isabel Allende

Dates refer to publication in United States.

The House of the Spirits, 1985

Of Love and Shadows, 1987

Eva Luna, 1988

The Stories of Eva Luna, 1989

The Infinite Plan, 1993

Paula, 1995

Aphrodite: A Memoir of the Senses, 1998

Daughter of Fortune, 1999

Portrait in Sepia, 2001

City of the Beasts, 2002

My Invented Country, 2003

Kingdom of the Golden Dragon, 2004

Zorro: A Novel, 2005

Forest of the Pygmies, 2005

Chapter Notes

CHAPTER 1. HELP FROM THE SPIRITS

1. Fernando González, "Latin America's Scheherazade," *Boston Globe*, April 25, 1993, p. 14.
2. Isabel Allende, *Paula* (New York: HarperCollins, translation 1995), p. 244.
3. Verónica Cortínez, "Isabel Allende," Carlos Solé, ed., *Latin American Writers, Supplement I* (New York: Charles Scribner's Sons, 2002), p. 10.
4. Isabel Allende, *The House of the Spirits* (New York: Bantam Books, 1986), p. 122.
5. Nora Erro-Peralta and Caridad Silva, eds., *Beyond the Border: A New Age in Latin American Women's Fiction*, (Gainesville: University Press of Florida, 2000), p. 1.
6. Cortínez, p. 6.
7. Hazel Rochman, "The Booklist Interview: Isabel Allende," *Booklist*, November 15, 2002, p. 591.
8. Isabel Allende, *Paula*, p. 278.
9. Celia Correas Zapata, *Isabel Allende: Life and Spirits* (Houston: Arte Público Press, 2002), pp. 44–45.
10. Erro-Peralta and Silva, p. 1.

CHAPTER 2. HOUSE OF SHADOWS

1. Isabel Allende, *Paula* (New York: HarperCollins, translation, 1995), p. 7.
2. Juan Andrés Piña, "The 'Uncontrollable' Rebel," *Conversaciones con la narrativa chilena* (Santiago, Chile:

Editorial Los Andes, 1991); reprinted in John Rodden, ed., *Conversations with Isabel Allende* (Austin, Tex.: University of Texas Press, 1999), p. 171.

3. Celia Correas Zapata, *Isabel Allende: Life and Spirits* (Houston: Arte Público Press, 2002), p. 3.

4. Allende, *Paula*, p. 28.

5. John Rodden, ed., "The Writer as Exile, and Her Search for Home," *Conversations with Isabel Allende* (Austin, Tex.: University of Texas Press, 1999), p. 432.

6. Isabel Allende, *My Invented Country* (New York: HarperCollins, translation, 2003), p. 68

7. Marjorie Agosín, "Pirate, Conjurer, Feminist," *Imagine 1*, no. 2 (Winter 1984), pp. 42–56; in Rodden, p. 40.

8. Zapata, p. 11.

9. Marie-Lise Gazarian Gautier, "If I Didn't Write, I Would Die," *Interviews with Latin American Writers* (Elmwood Park, Ill.: Dalkey Archive Press, 1989), pp. 5–24; in Rodden, p. 125.

10. Allende, *Paula*, p. 36.

11. Ibid., p. 33.

12. Ibid., p. 32.

13. Ibid., p. 44.

14. Ibid., p. 48.

Chapter 3. Adíos to Suecia Street

1. Isabel Allende, *Paula* (New York: HarperCollins, translation, 1995), pp. 58–59.

2. Ibid.

3. Bill Moyers, "Bill Moyers Interviews Isabel Allende," June 13, 2003, PBS transcript, p. 5, <http://www.pbs.org/now/transcript/transcript_allende.html> (August 8, 2003).

4. Allende, *Paula*, pp. 59–60.
5. Ibid., pp. 61–62.
6. Juan Andrés Piña, "The 'Uncontrollable' Rebel," *Conversaciones con la narrativa chilena* (Santiago, Chile: Editorial Los Andes, 1991); reprinted in John Rodden, ed., *Conversations with Isabel Allende* (Austin, Tex.: University of Texas Press, 1999), p. 168.
7. Ibid.
8. Ibid., p. 172.
9. Alvin P. Sanoff, "Modern Politics, Modern Fables," *U.S. News & World Report*, November 21, 1988; in Rodden, p. 103.
10. Allende, *Paula*, p. 63.
11. Ibid., p. 62.
12. Ibid., p. 86.
13. Rosemary G. Feal and Yvette E. Miller, eds., *Isabel Allende Today* (Pittsburgh, Pa.: Latin American Literary Review Press, 2002), p. 4.
14. Pina, p. 179.

CHAPTER 4. RETURN TO SUECIA STREET

1. Isabel Allende, *My Invented Country* (New York: HarperCollins, translation, 2003), p. 111.
2. Ibid., pp. 111, 114.
3. Juan Andrés Piña, "The 'Uncontrollable' Rebel," *Conversaciones con la narrativa chilena* (Santiago, Chile: Editorial Los Andes, 1991; reprinted in John Rodden, ed., *Conversations with Isabel Allende* (Austin, Tex.: University of Texas Press, 1999), p. 173.
4. Ibid., p. 170.
5. Ibid., p. 171.

6. Allende, *Paula* (New York: HarperCollins, translation, 1995), p. 119.
7. Pina, p. 174.
8. Ibid., pp. 173–174.
9. Allende, *Paula*, pp. 116, 117.
10. Katherine Martin, ed., *Women of Courage: Inspiring Stories from the Women Who Lived Them* (Novato, Calif.: New World Library, 1999), p. 5.
11. Bill Moyers, "Bill Moyers Interviews Isabel Allende," June 13, 2003, PBS transcript, p. 3, <http://www.pbs.org/now/transcript/transcript_allende.html> (August 8, 2003).

CHAPTER 5. FEMINIST AND REBEL

1. Verónica Cortínez, "Isabel Allende," in Carlos Solé, ed., *Latin American Writers, Supplement I* (New York: Charles Scribner's Sons, 2002), p. 3.
2. Ignacio Carrión, "Love and Tears," *El País Semanal*, November 28, 1993, pp. 48–59; in Rodden, pp. 301–302.
3. Ibid., p. 302.
4. Ibid.
5. Juan Andrés Piña, "The 'Uncontrollable' Rebel," *Conversaciones con la narrativa chilena* (Santiago, Chile: Editorial Los Andes, 1991); reprinted in John Rodden, ed., *Conversations with Isabel Allende* (Austin, Tex.: University of Texas Press, 1999), p. 179.
6. Ibid., p. 178.
7. Isabel Allende, *Paula* (New York: HarperCollins, translation 1995), p. 145.
8. Pina, p. 180.
9. "Introduction,"John Rodden, ed., *Conversations with Isabel Allende* (Austin, Tex.: University of Texas Press, 1999), p. 1.

10. Pina, pp. 181–182.

CHAPTER 6. FLIGHT INTO EXILE

1. Samuel Chavkin, *The Murder of Chile: Eyewitness Accounts of the Coup, the Terror, and the Resistance Today* (New York: Everest House Publishers, 1982), p. 1.
2. Ibid., p. 13.
3. Isabel Allende, *Paula* (New York: HarperCollins, translation 1995), p. 195.
4. Isabel Allende, "Speeches and Lectures," Isabel Allende Official Website, n.d., <http://www.isabelallende.com/index.html> (February 11, 2004).
5. Allende, *Paula*, p. 201.
6. Katherine Martin, ed., *Women of Courage: Inspiring Stories from the Women Who Lived Them* (Novato, Calif.: New World Library, 1999), p. 6.
7. Isabel Allende, *My Invented Country* (New York: HarperCollins, translation, 2003), p. 157.
8. Marjorie Agosín, "Pirate, Conjurer, Feminist," *Imagine 1*, no. 2 (Winter 1984): pp. 42–56; reprinted in John Rodden, ed., *Conversations with Isabel Allende* (Austin, Tex.: University of Texas Press, 1999), p. 39.
9. Ibid.
10. Celia Correas Zapata, *Isabel Allende: Life and Spirits* (Houston: Arte Público Press, 2002), p. 45.
11. Agosín, p. 41.
12. Juan Andrés Piña, "The 'Uncontrollable' Rebel," *Conversaciones con la narrativa chilena* (Santiago, Chile: Editorial Los Andes, 1991); in Rodden, p. 189.
13. "Porphyria Overview," American Porphyria Foundation, n.d., <http://www.porphyriafoundation.com/overview.html> (December 11, 2003).

CHAPTER 7. MAGICAL REALIST

1. Verónica Cortínez, "Isabel Allende," Carlos Solé, ed., *Latin American Writers, Supplement I* (New York: Charles Scribner's Sons, 2002), p. 7.

2. Ibid., p. 1.

3. Isabel Allende, "Writing as an Act of Hope," in William Zinsser, ed., *Paths of Resistance: The Art and Craft of the Political Novel* (Boston, Mass.: Houghton Mifflin, 1989), p. 50.

4. Virginia Invernizzi and Melissa Pope, "Women's Stories, My Stories," *Letras-femeninas*, Spring/Fall 1989, pp. 119–125; reprinted in John Rodden, ed., *Conversations with Isabel Allende* (Austin, Tex.: University of Texas Press, 1999), p. 122.

5. Ibid., p. 123.

6. Allende, "Writing as an Act of Hope," in Zinsser, p. 50.

7. Ibid.

8. Isabel Allende, "Foreword," in Rodden, p. x.

9. Ibid.

10. Elyse Crystall, Jill Kuhnheim, and Mary Layoun, "An Overwhelming Passion to Tell the Story," from *Contemporary Literature*, Winter 1992, pp. 585–600; in Rodden, p. 280.

11. Isabel Allende, *Paula* (New York: HarperCollins, translation, 1995), pp. 297–298.

12. Fernando González, "Latin America's Scheherazade," *Boston Globe*, April 25, 1993, p. 14.

13. Rosemary G. Feal and Yvette E. Miller, eds., *Isabel Allende Today* (Pittsburgh: Latin American Literary Review Press, 2002), p. 12.

14. Allende, *Paula*, p. 314.

15. Crystall, et al; in Rodden, p. 280.
16. Allende, *Paula*, p. 309.

CHAPTER 8. THE WRITER'S JOURNEY

1. Bill Moyers, "Bill Moyers Interviews Isabel Allende," June 13, 2003, PBS transcript, p. 3, <http://www.pbs.org/now/transcript/transcript_allende.html> (August 8, 2003).
2. Isabel Allende, *Paula* (New York: HarperCollins, translation, 1995), p. 3.
3. Katherine Martin, ed., *Women of Courage: Inspiring Stories from the Women Who Lived Them* (Novato, Calif.: New World Library, 1999), p. 8.
4. Ibid., p. 9.
5. Allende, *Paula*, pp. 309–310.
6. Ibid., p. 315.
7. Ibid., p. 329.
8. Martin, p. 9.
9. Ibid., p. 10.
10. Ignacio Carríon, "Love and Tears," El País Semanal, November 28, 1993, pp. 48–59; reprinted in John Rodden, ed., *Conversations with Isabel Allende* (Austin, Tex.: University of Texas Press, 1999), p. 307.
11. Allende, *Paula*, p. 300.
12. Alden Mudge, "Writing Home: Expatriate Isabel Allende Takes a New Look at Her Native Land," *Bookpage*, June 2003, p. 8.
13. Moyers, p. 3.
14. Judith Uyterlinde, "Spirits on the Big Screen," *Handelsblad* (Rotterdam, October 26, 1993); in Rodden, p. 295.
15. Michael Toms, "Writing From the Belly," *Common Boundary*, May/June 1994, pp. 16–23; in Rodden, p. 337.
16. Ibid., p. 338.

17. Robert Bly, *New York Times Book Review*, May 16, 1993, p. 13.
18. Kathryn Hughes, "Book Review of *The Infinite Plan*," *New Statesman & Society*, July 2, 1993, p. 38.
19. Merle Rubin, "Book Review of *The Infinite Plan*," *The Christian Science Monitor*, June 10, 1993, p. 14.

Chapter 9. The Most Generous Thing

1. Marjorie Rosen and Nancy Matsumoto, "Lady of the Spirits," *People Weekly*, May 2, 1994, p. 107.
2. Judith Uyterlinde, "Spirits on the Big Screen," Handelsblad (October 26, 1993), p. 6; reprinted in John Rodden, ed., *Conversations with Isabel Allende* (Austin, Tex.: University of Texas Press, 1999), p. 294.
3. Jennifer Benjamin and Sally Engelfried, "Magical Feminist," *East Bay Arts and Culture Magazine*, December 1994, pp. 18–19; in Rodden, p. 383.
4. Verónica Cortínez, "Isabel Allende," in Carlos Solé, ed., *Latin American Writers, Supplement I* (New York: Charles Scribner's Sons, 2002), p. 10.
5. Isabel Allende Foundation Website, n.d., <http://www.isabelallendefoundation.org/english/home.html> (January 27, 2004).
6. Ibid.
7. Ibid.
8. Isabel Allende, "On the Amazon: Snapshots of a Green Planet," *Salon*, April 1, 1997, <http://www.salon.com/march97/wanderlust/allende970325.html> (February 15, 2004).

9. "1998 Dorothy and Lillian Gish Prize to Be Awarded to Author Isabel Allende," *La Prensa San Diego*, September 25, 1998.

10. "The Frontrunner Awards," The Sara Lee Foundation Website, n.d., <http://www.saraleefoundation.org/history/awards_frontrunner.cfm> (January 29, 2004).

11. "Isabel Allende Discusses New Book on Sex and Food," CNN interactive, March 31, 1998, <http://www.cnn.com/books/dialogue/9803/isabel.allende/index.html> (December 12, 2003).

12. Isabel Allende, "Speeches and Lectures," Isabel Allende Official Website, n.d., <http://www.isabelallende.com/index.html> (February 11, 2004).

13. R. Z. Sheppard, "Footnotes No Longer: As Women's History Takes Root in the Canon, More Stories About the Past Take on a Female Voice," *Time*, November 15, 1999, p. 108.

14. Michiko Kakutani, "Books of the Times; A Single Girl Takes On the California Frontier," *The New York Times*, November 2, 1999, p. 7.

15. Daisy Maryles and Dick Donahue, "Fortunate Daughter," *Publishers Weekly*, February 21, 2000, p. 20.

16. Willa Cather, *O Pioneers!* As quoted by Christopher Vogler in *The Writer's Journey: Mythic Structure for Writers* (Studio City: Michael Wiese Productions, 1998), p. 9.

CHAPTER 10. MYSTERY AND MEMORY

1. Isabel Allende, *Portrait in Sepia* (New York: HarperCollins, 2002), p. 3.

2. Isabel Allende, "Foreword," in John Rodden, ed., *Conversations with Isabel Allende* (Austin, Tex.: University of Texas Press, 1999), p. x.

3. Isabel Allende, *My Invented Country* (New York: HarperCollins, translation, 2003), p. 179.

4. Alden Mudge, "Writing Home: Expatriate Isabel Allende Takes a New Look at Her Native Land," *Bookpage*, June 2003, p. 8.

5. Andrew Ervin, "Books in Brief: Fiction & Poetry; A Woman's Reconstruction," *The New York Times*, November 4, 2001, p. 32.

6. Nora Krug, "Book Review of *City of the Beasts*," *The New York Times*, February 9, 2003, p. 21.

7. Jane P. Fenn, "Review of Audiobook of *City of the Beasts*," *School Library Journal*, February 2003, p. 77.

8. "Book Review of *My Invented Country*," *Kirkus Reviews*, April 1, 2003, p. 514.

9. Allende, *My Invented Country*, pp. 9–10.

10. Bill Moyers, "Bill Moyers Interviews Isabel Allende," June 13, 2003, PBS transcript, p. 3, <http://www.pbs.org/now/transcript/transcript_allende.html> (August 8, 2003).

11. "Book Review of *Kingdom of the Golden Dragon*," *Kirkus Reviews*, April 1, 2004, p. 323.

12. Hazel Rochman, "Book Review of *Kingdom of the Golden Dragon*," *Booklist*, February 15, 2004, p. 1050.

13. "Book Review of *Kingdom of the Golden Dragon*," *Publishers Weekly*, March 15, 2004, p. 75.

14. Allende, *My Invented Country*, p. xii.

15. Ibid., p. 188.

16. Marie-Lise Gazarian Gautier, *Interviews with Latin American Writers* (Elmwood Park, Ill.: Dalkey Archive Press, 1989), reprinted in John Rodden, ed., *Conversations*

with Isabel Allende (Austin, Tex.: University of Texas Press, 1999), p. 130.

17. Isabel Allende, "Speeches and Lectures," Isabel Allende Official Website, n.d., <http://www.isabelallende.com/index.html> (February 11, 2004).

18. Ibid.

19. Virginia Invernizzi, "I Remember Emotion, I Remember Moments," in Rodden, p. 461.

Further Reading

Bloom, Harold, ed. *Isabel Allende* (Modern Critical Views). Philadelphia: Chelsea House Publishers, 2002.

Cox, Karen Castellucci, *Isabel Allende: A Critical Companion*. Westport, Conn.: Greenwood Publishing Group, 2003.

Levine, Linda Gould. *Isabel Allende*. Twayne Publishers, 2002.

Rodden, John, ed. *Conversations with Isabel Allende*. Austin: University of Texas Press, 1999.

Shirey, Lynn. *Latin American Writers*. New York: Facts on File, 1997.

Varona-Lacey, Gladys M. *Contemporary Latin-American Literature*. Chicago: McGraw Hill, 2001.

Zapata, Celia Correas. Translated by Margaret Sayers Peden. *Isabel Allende: Life and Spirits*. Houston, Texas: Arte Público Press, 2002.

Internet Addresses

Isabel Allende's Official Website

<http://www.isabelallende.com/index.htm>

Isabel Allende Foundation

<http://www.isabelallendefoundation.org/iaf.php>

Index

Page numbers for photographs are in **boldface** type.